LISTENING TO GOD

LISTENING TO GOD

USING SCRIPTURE AS A PATH TO GOD'S PRESENCE

Jan Johnson

NAVPRESS⦿

Bringing Truth to Life
NavPress Publishing Group
P.O. Box 35001, Colorado Springs, Colorado 80935

The Navigators is an international Christian organization. Our mission is to reach, disciple, and equip people to know Christ and to make Him known through successive generations. We envision multitudes of diverse people in the United States and every other nation who have a passionate love for Christ, live a lifestyle of sharing Christ's love, and multiply spiritual laborers among those without Christ.

NavPress is the publishing ministry of The Navigators. NavPress publications help believers learn biblical truth and apply what they learn to their lives and ministries. Our mission is to stimulate spiritual formation among our readers.

Cover art by Planet Art / Caillibotte

Some of the anecdotal illustrations in this book are true to life and are included with the permission of the persons involved. All other illustrations are composites of real situations, and any resemblance to people living or dead is coincidental.

Unless otherwise identified, all Scripture quotations in this publication are taken from the *HOLY BIBLE: NEW INTERNATIONAL VERSION* ® (NIV®). Copyright © 1973, 1978, 1984 by International Bible Society. Used by permission of Zondervan Publishing House. All rights reserved. Other versions used include: the *New Revised Standard Version* (NRSV), copyright 1989, by the Division of Christian Education of the National Council of the Churches of Christ in the USA, used by permission, all rights reserved; and the *King James Version* (KJV).

Printed in the United States of America

1 2 3 4 5 6 7 8 9 10 11 12 13 14 15 / 99 98 97

FOR A FREE CATALOG OF
NAVPRESS BOOKS & BIBLE STUDIES,
CALL 1-800-366-7788 (USA)
OR 1-416-499-4615 (CANADA)

To my mother,
Kay Karsten,
who taught me to love Scripture
when I was a little girl.

Contents

PART ONE
Finding Intimacy with God
When You Need to Sense God's Love and Acceptance

PART TWO
Making Progress in the Spiritual Life
When You Want to Let God Change You

PART THREE
Healing Life's Wounds
When You Sense God Speaking to Your Deeper Hurts

PART FOUR
Having the Heart of Christ
When God Calls You to Be Different from Others

PART FIVE
Building Relationships
When You'd Like to Connect Better with Others

PART SIX
Moving Beyond Mediocrity
When You Want to Discern God's Purpose for Your Life

Introduction

How Contemplative Bible Studies Differ from Other Bible Studies

Most of us spend years in school reading textbooks to gather facts we can later display on a test. We may use Bible study guides the same way — digging out facts about God and storing them for later use. The problem is that knowing facts doesn't always change the way we relate to God. The Bible itself suggests that knowing biblical facts is not enough to change our lives; what we need is to meditate on God's works, reflect on who God is, and consider His mighty deeds (Joshua 1:8; Psalm 77:12). Through meditation on passages of Scripture, we can seek God and come to know Him. And God changes us through this experience.

The goal of these Bible study meditations is to assist you in surrendering yourself to God and asking Him to put in your heart what He wants you to know, understand, and obey about His will. As you cooperate with God, using the time-proven methods of devotional Bible reading and meditating, He is likely to speak to you. Your prayers during the study, and in subsequent moments of the day, give you an opportunity to ponder the message you've read and, if necessary, wrestle with God about how in the world He might ever accomplish this message in you.

This type of study and meditation may be different from what you're used to. Consider this comparison between Bible study and meditation:

IN THE "STUDY" METHOD, YOU . . .	IN THE "MEDITATION" METHOD, YOU . . .

■ dissect the text
■ ask questions about the text
■ read and compare facts and new
  ways of applying facts
	■ savor the text and enter into it
	■ let the text ask questions of you
	■ read to let God speak to you (in
	  light of facts already absorbed).

To prepare you for meditation, these studies examine historical, linguistic, and cultural facts that provide clues to help you understand what was intended by the writer of the text. Within that accurate textual rendering, you can discern what God may be saying to you on this day, in this moment of your life. God may be urging you to consider a new idea; He may be questioning your motives; or He may be reminding you of ways He has worked in your life in the past. The goal of this study is to discern what God is saying to you.

You may wonder, *Am I putting words in God's mouth? Am I making this up?* The obvious answers include that God doesn't say anything that's out of sync with His commands (to not kill or exploit someone, for example) or who He is (full of integrity and mercy).

Here are some common ways we read our own thoughts into the text.

■ We manipulate our senses to "hear" God say what we (at some level) want Him to say. For example, while meditating on James and John's mother's inappropriate request to her sons, you decide this is a message that your mother lacks discernment and you should discount what she just told you the previous day.

- We read into the text ideas that people have told us about ourselves. For example, your friend keeps telling you to be more patient, so you're likely to read that message into almost any Bible narrative. Yes, it's good to be patient, but perhaps God has something else to say to you today.
- We apply the text in ways we've heard it taught previously. We think we know what the passage is about before we really delve into it. This can be a problem, especially if you've studied the passage before or if it's a favorite passage. For example, I heard a sermon in college on Philippians 4:4-8 ("Rejoice in the Lord always"), in which I was told that this passage is a "formula for happiness." Only with a great deal of effort have I set aside that idea and been able to examine what those verses mean and how they relate to my life situation today.

When we put words in God's mouth, we replace an encounter with the living, productive, penetrating Word of God with our own ideas. If you are normally sharp and quick-thinking in Bible study, this may be especially challenging for you. You may be anxious to pour out your thoughts before they're fully baked in the oven of silence. It's better to sit with them and let the yeast take its full effect.

If you think you might be controlling the meditation, ask yourself: *Am I writing the script or am I receiving it? Am I able to be surprised by what comes to me?* You can help yourself let go of control by paying attention to the details of the setting and culture — the role of shepherds, what the grasslands Jacob slept in were like. These details immerse us in the text and distract us from turning it into a sermon.

If you find yourself forcing something artificial on the text, admit it, set the thought aside, and ask God, *What else?* If nothing else comes, hold on to your idea and wait. You will know the authenticity of it by its fruit. If you did force the thought, was the time spent meditating wasted? No, you are learning communication skills with the heavenly Father. The next time you think you hear the Shepherd's voice (John 10:3-4), your ears will be a little sharper.

As you become skilled at setting aside your conclusions, the more common problem will be a sorrowful conviction: *God did say this to me, and I must die to myself in order to follow it!* It requires a surrender of the will to let God speak to you in a fresh way and question who you are.

By allowing the text to question you, you are less likely to do as the person described in James 1:22-25, who looked in the mirror but walked away and forgot what he looked like. Instead, this method — a version of an ancient method called *lectio divina* (sacred reading) — invites you to "[look] intently into the perfect law that gives freedom." He or she who "continues to do this, not forgetting what he has heard, but doing it — he will be blessed in what he does" (verse 25).

These meditations can be used over and over because you are changing and growing, which means the reflection in the mirror changes. That's not to say that God or the Scripture changes, but the parts of yourself you bring to it change. You can meditate on the same Scripture passages again and again because the truths they communicate will affect different areas of your life. That is, the next time you meditate on the passage you focused on today, you will be undergoing different difficulties, involved in different causes, or have come to a new place of under-standing with God. It's not that the passage will speak differently (although different aspects may emerge), but you will be different. As a result, the Scripture will be ever fresh and new, offering God's words to you.

Whether done in a group or individually, these studies require a quieting of the self so that you may detach mentally from others for several moments of silence and then reflect on what God may be saying to you. This will build your skill at hearing God at the heart and soul level. You will learn to ask yourself, *How do I react to the text? How do I respond deep within? Why do I have these thoughts?* God is actually quite current in your life, and He will speak to your broken places — the ones you are aware of and others you may not be aware of. *Lectio divina* challenges you to let an infinite, all-powerful God tiptoe into the messy realities of your life and offer words of wisdom, comfort, and confrontation.

Guidelines for Personal Meditation

1. Find a place that is quiet and isolated. Disconnect the telephone if necessary. The most common position for meditating is to sit in a chair with a straight back, placing your feet flat on the floor and your hands either gently clasped or placed on your knees. Find a sitting position in which you can get settled and stay there. This will decrease distractions and help you stay on track. If you cross your arms or legs, at some point they'll need to be uncrossed, and you'll get distracted, thinking, *Should I uncross my leg now or wait? What if my leg falls asleep?*
2. Relax by taking several slow, deep breaths and relaxing your shoulders and legs. No matter how practiced you are, this is important to do every time.
3. Notice the stillness and enjoy it. Remember that God is gazing at you with great love.
4. Ponder the passage presented to you. Picture it, taste it, hear it, live in it. When your mind wanders, don't be discouraged. Gently come back to the passage. You may wish to set a timer to remind yourself when to start the next step. (Instructions to group leaders are in shaded boxes and marked with the symbol ❶, but you can ignore them when working by yourself.)
5. Don't get upset if it seems as if nothing comes to you, especially during the "Pondering the Invitation" portion. Something may come to you later, or this may have been a time for you to just sit and enjoy God's presence.
6. At the end of your meditation, you may wish to write down your thoughts in a journal or discuss the experience with a friend.

Guidelines for Group Meditation

1. Meet to discuss procedures as a group. Address such questions as these:

   - How many sessions do we want to have? These studies are geared for weekly meetings, but does that work for the whole group?
   - Which sections of meditations will we use?
   - How much time will we allow for each session? (The meditations are designed for a ninety-minute session but can be modified.)
   - Where will we meet? If possible, meet in the same place every week. If child

care will be provided, it's helpful to have the children at another site.
■ Will leadership rotate among all group members, or will one person lead the group? If possible, change leaders weekly. Good leaders are not experts; they are those who are willing to be themselves and are open to God's Spirit.

Besides using the instructions for leaders (in shaded boxes marked with the symbol ❶), use as much of the instructions to individuals as you wish. You may also have to help participants stay on track or within the structure: "Only two sentences, please." If you're not used to silent meditation, time yourself. Each time the instructions say "sit quietly together," allow at least two minutes. For "Soaking In the Passage" and "Pondering the Invitation" sections, five minutes is appropriate. If this is difficult at first, help the group work up to it.

■ May newcomers join? If none of you has done meditation in groups before, your group might want to work it out together before inviting more people.

2. Discuss group participation guidelines: (You may wish to read these at the beginning of each group meeting.)

■ *Openness*—I will be as candid and honest as I am able. I understand this group is a safe place in which I can admit strong emotions, confess distasteful faults, and reveal insights that seem outlandish.
■ *Confidentiality*—I will not tell anyone outside the group what someone else said in the group—not even spouses or absent group members. I may tell someone what I said, but not what someone else said.
■ *Acceptance*—I will avoid judging, giving advice, or criticizing, even if it's only in my mind—*He's way off! She's never going to plug into this meditation!* I will try to turn this self-talk into a prayer for the person or situation and then focus on the passage in front of me.
■ *Talking within the group*—I understand that this study is different from discussion Bible studies. I come together with others not to have extended conversation but for the community experience of seeking God. I abide by instructions to say only a word or two.
    If I don't like the format, I can ask the group to set aside time at the end for group discussion. If something about the passage bothers me, I can discuss that with someone else later. (Some baffling points are dealt with in "Reading the Passage" to help participants look at them and move on.)
■ *Wonder*—I expect other group members to sense insights that are different from mine. At those times I may wonder, *Did they read the same passage?* I will reaffirm that God meets each of us in the places that still need to conform to the image of Christ. For each of us, those places are different. I will enjoy the wonder of how God speaks to each of us as special children.
■ *Uniquenesses*—I will make allowances for differences in temperament, timing, and needs. Some people resonate better with passages about metaphors and images; others relate better to Bible characters; still others like the silence best.
■ *Privacy*—If I am unable to answer a question aloud because no answer comes to me, or I'm unwilling to reveal my answer to the group, I may say, "Pass," and offer no explanation.

■ *Attentiveness*—I will try to attend the group meetings and be open to the needs of others when I am there.

You may add to or revise these guidelines. As a group leader, don't hesitate to remind participants gently of a guideline during the session, if necessary.

The Important Skill of Centering Yourself during Quiet Moments

Whether you do the meditations alone or with others, you may find the silence disturbing. You may think, *What if my mind can't stop racing? What do I do to remove the obstacles that get in my way? What if I get bored?*

Each session leads you in a quiet time. You are guided in quieting your thoughts and inner activity, and in paying attention to the presence of God. Nevertheless, it's sometimes difficult to throw off thoughts about the doughnut shop you passed earlier or who might telephone you while you're away from home. If you let these obstacles take control over your meditation, you become like the rocky ground into which seeds fall, but the plants wither quickly in the shallow soil (Matthew 13:5-6). It can be a struggle to detach from the world in order to attach to God. But it's worth it to learn how to be still and know that God is God.

As you settle down, this exercise, or a similar one, might help:

Begin by placing your palms down as a symbolic indication of your desire to turn over to God any concerns or distractions you may have. Inwardly, you may pray, "Lord, I give to you my anger toward John. I release my fear of my dentist appointment this morning. I surrender my anxiety over not having enough money to pay the bills this month. I release my frustration over trying to find a baby-sitter for tonight." Whatever is a concern to you, just say, "Palms down." Release it. After several moments of surrender, turn your palms up as a symbol of your desire to receive from the Lord. Perhaps you will pray silently: "Lord, I would like to receive your divine love for John, your peace about the dentist appointment, your patience, your joy."[1]

You may wish to jot down the things that distract you—errands to run, people to call—so that you can release them for a few moments. The more you practice quieting yourself, the easier it becomes each time. It takes some discipline at first, but once you begin adjusting to God's wavelength, expect to enjoy abiding there. The quiet will renew you, not bore you. When words are spoken, they have more value and weight because silence is so prized.

Centering your thoughts is a step of faith, a sign that you are open to what is unknown to you but known to God. In our world of considering options, exploring avenues, and investigating theories, we have sought to know as much as we can. Centering is a ridiculously helpless statement that God can work, and we can simply watch in awe.

---

1. Richard Foster, *Celebration of Discipline* (San Francisco: Harper & Row, 1988), pp. 30-31.

PART ONE

FINDING INTIMACY WITH GOD

When You Need to Sense God's Love and Acceptance

So, What Is *Lectio Divina?*

Traditional *lectio divina* involves four phases: reading (*lectio*), meditation (*meditatio*), prayer (*oratio*), and contemplation (*contemplatio*). Reading and prayer are familiar to many, but the other two are not. Meditation is that rambling reasoning process in which words and events are prayerfully pondered, thereby opening the possibility of drawing personal meaning from them. Contemplation is a focused resting in God in which words become less important than the fellowship with the Father[1].

Lectio divina, then, engages the whole person: mind, heart, and spirit, intellect and imagination, will and affections. The studies in this book will help you do this as you "chew" on Scripture. To make God's Word a part of yourself, Scripture needs to be turned over, puzzled, and wrestled with until you find yourself face-to-face with God. In the days afterward, the truth replays itself.

This is not for the spiritually elite. In fact, people who don't like traditional Bible study often find *lectio divina* helpful. Christians have practiced it for hundreds of years, as many now do all over the world, including in places such as Africa and Latin America.[2]

In the format suggested in this study, the order of prayer and contemplation are reversed. Contemplation is focused in the "Soaking In the Passage" section as we ask God to show us how our lives are touched today. In truth, all four phases overlap, which is a precedent for life — work and meditation, exercise and prayer, sleeping and contemplation are all interwoven.

The repetition of reading the Scripture isn't a waste of time. Even if you're by yourself, read it aloud at least once. When your physical ear hears the words, it creates a resonance that stays with you. It breaks up the familiar singsong and causes words and phrases to stand out. With those chosen words and phrases, you can form questions for God that keep you in constant conversation with Him all day long.

---

1. Thelma Hall, *Too Deep for Words: Rediscovering Lectio Divina* (New York: Paulist Press, 1988), p. 9.
2. Norvene Vest, *Bible Reading for Spiritual Growth* (San Francisco, Calif.: Harper San Francisco, 1993), p. 95.

Knowing I'm Loved

Luke 15:1-7

Warming Up   5-10 minutes

Reflect in silence for at least two minutes. To help center yourself, try the following:

- Breathe in and out deeply five or six times. Relax your neck and move it around. Let your arms go limp and relax your legs and ankles. Relax each part from the inside out.
- If you have trouble quieting yourself, try using the "palms down, palms up" method. Rest your hands in your lap, placing the palms down whenever you think of concerns you need to turn over to God. Turn your palms up as a symbol of your desire to receive from the Lord and set aside distractions.

Ask yourself the following quiet question to help focus your thoughts for meditation on today's passage: What does it feel like to be found when you've been lost?

Take a few minutes to reflect on the question. It's okay if nothing comes to mind right away. Just enjoy God's presence.

Reading the Passage   15-20 minutes

Read the following Scripture passage, noting the explanations in the shaded box below the passage.

Luke 15:1-7

THE CRITICISM

¹Now the tax collectors and "sinners" were all gathering around to hear him. ²But the Pharisees and the teachers of the law muttered, "This man welcomes *sinners* and eats with them."

THE RESPONSE

³Then Jesus told them this parable: ⁴"Suppose one of you has a hundred sheep and loses one of them. Does he not *leave the ninety-nine in the open country* and go after the lost sheep until he finds it? ⁵And when he finds it, he joyfully puts it on his shoulders ⁶and goes home. Then he calls his friends and neighbors together and says, 'Rejoice with me; I have found my lost sheep.' ⁷ I tell you that in the same way there is more rejoicing in heaven over one sinner who repents than over ninety-nine righteous persons who do not need to repent."

If you haven't read the notes in the shaded box, read them now. Take a minute to consider the following questions.

❶ After the passage is read aloud, ask group members to read the explanations in the shaded box and jot down answers to the following questions. After a few minutes, ask group members to choose one question and share their answer in a sentence or two. Explain that this is not a time for discussion but for reporting responses to the questions. Anyone who wishes to pass may do so.

The Eager, Enthusiastic Shepherd

1. Look through the Scripture passage above and underline phrases that show the eagerness and enthusiasm of the shepherd. Here are two examples to get you started: "go after the lost sheep" (verse 4); "joyfully puts it on his shoulders" (verse 5).

Sinners—Pharisees had no social or business dealings with those they called the "people of the land." They considered these people "sinners" because they didn't keep the Law.[1]

Leave the ninety-nine in the open country—Many commentators suggest the shepherd didn't abandon the ninety-nine but left them in a sheepfold or with another shepherd. The text, however, speaks of leaving them in open country and mentions no other shepherd. Jesus may have intended for the rash behavior of the shepherd to underscore the theme that God pursues each person madly and passionately. If so, this story would have been a shocking comeback to the Pharisees, who didn't like Jesus associating at all with sinners, much less the idea of God running off to save them.

The Criticism and the Response

2. Jesus told this parable to respond to the criticism of the Pharisees that He ate with tax collectors and "sinners." Contrast the shepherd's behavior with the Pharisees' behavior.

The Pharisees were eager to:

The shepherd was eager to:

3. What do you think Jesus was trying to say through this parable to the Pharisees who criticized Him for eating with tax collectors and "sinners"?

4. Read "Cultural Cue: The Heart of the Shepherd" below. When have you had that kind of heart—a heart that searches earnestly for someone or something?

5. In what situations, if any, do you wish God would "find" you and restore you to tranquility?

If any of the above questions are too difficult, hold them before God for a few minutes and then go on. Don't worry about getting an answer, but be open to what may come to mind in the next few days.

Picturing the Passage   10-15 minutes

Before reading the passage again, consider the Cultural Cue and use it to set the scene for this scriptural passage.

> ❶ Have group members read this cue silently, then ask a group member to read the passage aloud while the others picture the passage.

Cultural Cue: The Heart of the Shepherd

Sheepherder Phillip Keller, who has spent many hours searching for lost sheep, explains that if a sheep falls onto its back and can't right itself, it becomes "cast." As it lies on its back, gases build up in its belly and blood circulation is cut off. It struggles frantically to get up. If the shepherd doesn't find the sheep in time, it will die. Keller says, "This is another reason why it is essential for a careful sheepman to look over his flock every day. If one or two are missing, often the first thought to flash into the shepherd's mind is, *One of my sheep is cast somewhere. I must go in search and set it on its feet again.*"[2]

Read the passage again—aloud this time—and close your eyes. Keep in mind the distinctive call of the shepherd to which the sheep recognize and respond. This is the voice that guides them to their watering place every day; this is the shepherd whose staff untangles them from brambles and wild roses, whose voice brings them to shelter before a storm hits.

Soaking In the Passage   5-15 minutes

Consider the all-important question you should ask whenever you read Scripture: How is my life touched today by this passage? Read the passage aloud again and ponder the following question for about five minutes: *What word, phrase, scene, or image emerges from the Scripture and stays with me?* If you latch on to something right away, set that aside for a minute and see if anything else emerges.

Here are some examples of scenes or images that might come to mind:

- the shepherd looking for the lost sheep
- the lost sheep found (you may wish to picture the shepherd carrying you on his shoulders)
- one of the ninety-nine sheep left in the open country (you may wish to picture the shepherd continuing to search in the rain for the lost sheep)

After a few minutes, write the word or phrase or image from the passage that resonates within you.

Word or phrase:

Scene or image: I hear . . . I see . . .

🕐 Ask a different group member to read the passage aloud and then state the question printed in italics above. After the group members reflect inwardly for a few moments, have them write the word or phrase or image that comes to mind. After a few minutes, ask group members to read what they've written, or pass, if they wish to.

Pondering the Invitation   5-15 minutes

Perhaps God is offering you an invitation in this passage to enlarge your understanding. In what way might that be? Sit quietly for a few minutes and ponder this question: *What do I need to know from this passage?* Be open to the quietness, but don't feel pressured to come up with an answer.

❶ Read the above instructions aloud. After a few minutes, repeat the question printed in italics. Ask group members to respond by saying, "I sense this passage calling me to . . . ." Then complete the statement with a short phrase. Anyone who wishes to pass may do so. Encourage members to listen respectfully and prayerfully to other group members.

Praying   5-10 minutes

Take a few minutes to respond to God. How do you feel about what you sensed (or didn't sense) during this time of reflection? What is it you most want to say to God right now?

❶ After allowing a few minutes for private prayer, ask group members to pray for the person on their left, according to that person's response in "Pondering the Invitation." Anyone wishing to pray silently may do so by saying, "I'm praying silently," and signifying when he or she is finished by saying, "Amen."

Daily Lectio

If you wish, use the above format to meditate on God's Word between group meetings. You may want to focus on today's passage every day this week, or you can use the following passages for meditation. (Try reading a different version of the Bible than NIV.)

- Psalm 119:168-176 (how a stray sheep behaves upon return)
- Ezekiel 34:12-16 (God brings back strays)
- Luke 15:8-10 (the woman's persistent search for the coin)
- John 10:11-17 (Jesus as the Good Shepherd)
- 1 Peter 2:21-25 (walking in the steps of the Shepherd and Overseer)
- Revelation 7:16-17 (a time when the Lamb is Shepherd, and no one will ever thirst)

---

1. William Barclay, *The Daily Bible Study: The Gospel of Luke* (Philadelphia: Westminster Press, 1956), p. 206.
2. Phillip Keller, *A Shepherd Looks at Psalm 23* (Grand Rapids, Mich.: Zondervan, 1970), pp. 60-61 of large print edition.

Christ Accepts Me

Romans 5:1-2,6-8

❶ After group members have greeted one another, ask them to close their eyes, relax their muscles, and breathe deeply. Then present the quiet question in the "Warming Up" section and let them reflect silently for a few minutes. Repeat the question and ask them to share their thoughts in a sentence or two. Anyone who wishes to pass may do so.

Warming Up   5-10 minutes
Center yourself by breathing in and out deeply several times. Bend your neck back and forth, and then let the muscles in your arms, hands, legs, and feet go limp. Release each distraction, one by one.

When you are relaxed, consider this quiet question: When has it been most clear to you (if ever) that God accepts you? If an answer doesn't come at this time, that's fine. Simply enjoy sitting in God's presence.

Reading the Passage   15-20 minutes
Silently read the following passage, noting the explanations in the shaded box at the bottom of the page.

❶ Ask a group member to read the passage aloud. Suggest that other group members close their eyes as they listen.

Romans 5:1-2, 6-8

GOD'S OFFER

[1]Therefore, since we have been *justified* through faith, we have peace with God through our Lord Jesus Christ, [2]through whom we have gained access by faith into this grace in which we now stand.

WHY IT CAN WORK

[6]You see, at just the right time, when we were still powerless, Christ died for the ungodly. [7]Very rarely will anyone die for a righteous man, though for a good man someone might possibly dare to die. [8]But God demonstrates his own love for us in this: While we were *still sinners,* Christ died for us.

If you haven't read the notes in the shaded box below, read them now. Take a minute to consider the following questions.

> ❶ After the passage is read, ask group members to read the explanations in the shaded box below and jot down answers to the questions below. After a few minutes, ask them to choose one question and share their answer in a sentence or two. Anyone who wishes to pass may do so. Explain that this is not a time for discussion but for reporting responses to the questions.

Passage Theme

1. Which of the following do you need most? (Rate them 1-4, 1 being the most needed.)

___ a sense of being justified—that I'm okay before God
___ peace with God
___ faith in God
___ a sense of God's grace, that He loves me, regardless of my mistakes

---

Justified—Made right in God's eyes, even though we don't live perfectly; having a broken bone set perfectly and then mended so well that you can't tell it was ever broken.

Still sinners—God doesn't wait until we become godly creatures before He loves us or helps us. He loves us as we are, even before we turn to Him.

2. When you think *I really blew it this time — God must be mad at me now!* what does this passage say to you about:

how God accepts you?

how God equips you to move forward?

3. In what situations do you feel most powerless (verse 6)?

4. How has God demonstrated His love to you recently?

Picturing the Passage   10-15 minutes
Before reading the Bible passage again, consider the following Character Cue.

Character Cue: The Apostle Paul, Chief of Sinners
Writing to Timothy, his friend and partner, Paul said, "Christ Jesus came into the world to save sinners; of whom I am chief" (1 Timothy 1:15, KJV). Before Paul became a Christian, he was a mass murderer of Christians, going from house to house and dragging off men and women to put them in prison. His mission? "To destroy the church" (Acts 8:3).

When we realize that God spoke the words in today's Scripture passage through the mouth of a person who ordered the deaths of so many people, certain words in the passage take on new passion:

- *justified*: Can such a sinner ever be justified?
- *peace*: Can God really be at peace with such a person? Can that person ever be at peace with himself?
- *grace*: Is there enough grace in God to forgive such a man as Paul?
- *ungodly*: This is a perfect description of Paul's actions.
- *sinners*: The word *sinner* describes Paul, and in that state, Christ died for him.

Now read the passage aloud and close your eyes. If you wish, use the following idea to picture a scene from this passage. The phrase "gained access" (verse 2) in the original biblical language carries with it the idea of being introduced into the presence and the chamber of the king.[1] Picture, for a moment, being ushered by Christ into the physical presence of God (Ephesians 2:18, 3:12).

Based on the Bible passage, what words might Christ use to introduce Paul to God? To introduce you to God? How would God respond? For example:

■ Christ might say to God about you, "Here is my friend who is powerless to save herself". (verse 6)
■ God might respond: "I am here for you. You and I have peace together". (verse 1)

As you picture yourself being introduced to God, read the passage aloud and then close your eyes, picking out a few phrases that would be appropriate to the scene. If you wish, use your ideas to fill in the blanks below:

How Jesus introduces me:

How God responds:

❶ Have group members read the character cue, then ask a group member to read the passage aloud while the others picture the introductions. After a few minutes, ask group members to describe in a sentence or two what they pictured. Anyone who wishes to pass may do so.

Soaking In the Passage   5-15 minutes

Ask yourself: How does the truth of this passage touch my life today? Read the passage aloud again and ponder the following question for several minutes: *Is there one word or phrase in this passage that speaks to me and stays with me?* After a few minutes, write down the word or phrase that resonates within you.

❶ Ask a different group member to read the passage aloud and then state the question printed in italics. Ask the group to fill in the word or phrase that sticks with them. After a few minutes, ask group members to read what they've written. Anyone who wishes to pass may do so.

Word or phrase:

Pondering the Invitation   5-15 minutes

Perhaps God is offering you an invitation in this passage to do or be something within the next few days. What might that be? Sit quietly for a few minutes, pondering this question: *What do I sense this passage telling me that I need to know in a fuller sense?* Be open to the quietness, but don't feel pressured to come up with something.

❶ Read the above instructions aloud and repeat the question printed in italics. Ask group members to respond by saying, "I sense this passage calling me to . . . ." Then complete that statement with a short phrase. Anyone who wishes to pass may do so.

Praying   5-10 minutes

Respond to God by telling Him how you feel about what you sensed or didn't sense during this meditation. If you need to present questions to God, do so.

❶ After allowing a few minutes for private prayer, ask group members to pray for the person on their left. Anyone wishing to pray silently may do so by saying, "I'm praying silently," and signifying when he or she is finished by saying "Amen."

Daily Lectio

If you wish, use the above format to meditate on God's Word between group meetings. You may wish to focus on today's passage every day this week, or you may use the following passages:

- Psalm 21:1-7 (rejoicing in God's strength and unfailing love)
- Luke 7:3-10 (a centurion who didn't deserve to have Jesus come)
- Romans 8:1-5 (living by the Holy Spirit's power instead of living by our sinful nature)
- Ephesians 2:14-18 (Christ makes peace between enemies and gives both sides access to God)
- 1 Timothy 1:13-17 (Paul's experience of grace and love)
- Jude 24-25 (joy in God's presence)

---

1. D. Guthrie and J. A. Motyer, *The New Bible Commentary* (Grand Rapids, Mich.: Eerdmans, 1991), p. 1024.

Loved, No Matter What

Luke 15:11-24

❶ After group members have had a chance to greet each other, read the centering instructions below. Then present the quiet question and let them reflect silently for a few minutes. Repeat the question and ask them to share their thoughts in a sentence or two. Anyone who wishes to pass may do so.

Warming Up   5-10 minutes

Center yourself by breathing in and out several times. Bend your neck back and forth and then take time to let your muscles relax. Turn over each distraction as needed. Once you feel quieted, ask yourself the following question to help focus your thoughts for meditation on today's passage: When have you recently sensed God running toward you?

Close your eyes and take a few minutes to consider the events of the week — conversations with friends or books you've read — to see if anything comes to you. If nothing comes to mind, simply enjoy God's presence.

Reading the Passage   15-20 minutes

As you read the Bible passage below, the story may sound familiar to you. Try to set aside what you know about it and read each word with fresh eyes. Note the explanations in the shaded box.

❶ Ask a group member to read the Bible passage aloud. Suggest that other group members close their eyes as they listen.

Luke 15:11-24

A WILD IDEA

[11]Jesus continued: "There was a man who had two sons. [12]The younger one said to his father, 'Father, *give me my share of the estate.*' So he divided his property between them.

[13]"Not long after that, the younger son got together all he had, set off for a distant country and there squandered his wealth in wild living.

WILD LIVING

[14]"After he had spent everything, there was a severe famine in that whole country, and he began to be in need. [15]So he went and hired himself out to a citizen of that country, who sent him to his fields to feed pigs. [16]He longed to fill his stomach with the *pods that the pigs were eating,* but no one gave him anything.

[17]"When he came to his senses, he said, 'How many of my father's hired men have food to spare, and here I am starving to death! [18]I will set out and go back to my father and say to him: Father, I have sinned against heaven and against you. [19]I am no longer worthy to be called your son; make me like one of your hired men.'"

A WILD RESPONSE

[20]So he got up and went to his father.

"But *while he was still a long way off,* his father saw him and was filled with compassion for him; he ran to his son, threw his arms around him and kissed him.

[21]"The son said to him, 'Father, I have sinned against heaven and against you. I am no longer worthy to be called your son.'

Give me my share of the estate — This was the same as saying, "Dad, let's pretend you're dead. I'll take my half now." The boy could have been executed for such rebellious behavior (Deuteronomy 21:18-21).

My share — This would have been one-third of the estate, since the oldest son got a double portion. (Deuteronomy 21:17)

The pods that the pigs were eating — Since the storyteller was Jewish and was speaking to a Jewish audience, we might assume the boy in the story is a Jew who is feeding pigs and eating their food. Jews did not eat or sacrifice pigs, and usually wouldn't touch them. This boy appears to have sunk so low as to have violated his faith.

While he was still a long way off — The text doesn't say how the father could see the boy when he was far away. Did he have servants posted on the perimeter of his land? Did he stand on his roof for years? Did he have friends in town who sped off to alert him? Or, did Jesus attribute to the father his own miraculous powers to see His disciples struggling from many miles away (Mark 6:46-48)?

[22]"But the father said to his servants, 'Quick! Bring the best robe and put it on him. Put a ring on his finger and sandals on his feet. [23]Bring the fattened calf and kill it. Let's have a feast and celebrate. [24]For this son of mine was dead and is alive again; he was lost and is found.' So they began to celebrate."

If you haven't read the notes in the shaded boxes, read them now. Take a minute to consider the following questions.

❶ After the passage is read aloud, ask group members to read silently the explanations in the shaded boxes and then jot down answers to the questions below. After a few minutes, ask them to choose one question and share their answer in a sentence or two. Anyone who wishes to pass may do so. Explain that this is not a time for discussion but for reporting responses to the questions.

Wild Plot Twists

1. What do you find most moving about the father's behavior?

   ☐ that he didn't stop his son, but let the boy figure things out on his own
   ☐ that he kept watching for the boy
   ☐ that he wouldn't even let the boy confess what he had done wrong
   ☐ that he gave the boy such honor and authority after he proved he didn't deserve it
   ☐ other:

2. What one word would you use to describe the father's behavior? For example, *selfless, eager, lavish?*

3. What needs of the boy did the father meet by giving him honor (a robe), authority (the signet ring), necessary goods (sandals, perhaps because he had bare feet), and a party (killing the fattened calf)?

   ☐ The father made it look like the boy fit in at this auspicious home.
   ☐ The father reassured the boy of his love.
   ☐ The father returned the boy's dignity to him.
   ☐ Other:

4. When have you struck out on your own in some way (making a decision, pursuing a relationship, or striking an attitude) and then wondered if it would really work to return to God or His ways?

5. Is there an empty, unproductive "land of famine" from which you need to return? If so, what is that land?

Picturing the Passage
10-15 minutes

Before reading the passage again, consider the following cues.

Cultural Cue: The Son's Robe

As the boy headed home, he probably wore a coarse, tattered garment that swine-herders customarily wore. The father offered him more than the conventional outer cloak; he clothed him in a long, flowing, elaborate garment, or *stole*, (the same garment inhabitants of heaven will wear; see Revelation 6:11).[1]

Character Cue: Jesus as a Shocking Storyteller

Today, speakers often tell stories that make people say to themselves, *I feel just like that.* Jesus did the opposite. He opened people's eyes by telling parables based on shocking, preposterous ideas—a Samaritan caring for a Jew; homes built on sand; leaving ninety-nine sheep in open country to search for one lost sheep. The parable of the prodigal son is based on a shocking premise—a son saying to a father, "Let's pretend you're dead so you can give me my portion now." Yet in this shocking story, we clearly see our predicament.

Read the passage again—aloud this time. Pick one or more of the scenes below and apply these questions: What do you think is going on inside the father? Inside the boy? What expressions might have been on their faces?

☐ the boy asking for his inheritance
☐ the boy living a wild life, then reduced to eating pods
☐ the father running down the trail to embrace the boy
☐ the father and the boy standing next to each other

❶ Have group members read these cues silently. Then have a group member read the passage aloud and ask the others to picture one or more of the scenes.

Soaking In the Passage
5-15 minutes

Reflect on how your life is touched by this passage today. Read the passage aloud again and ponder the following question: *What special dramatic moment, scene, word, or phrase emerges from the passage and stays with me?*

After a few minutes, write the word, phrase, moment, or scene that resonates within you.

Word or phrase:

Dramatic moment or scene: I hear . . . I see . . .

❶ Ask a different group member to read the passage aloud, then state the question printed in italics. Have the group think about the word, phrase, moment, or scene that stays with them and record it in the space provided. After a few minutes, ask people to read what they've written. Anyone who wishes to pass may do so.

Pondering the Invitation   5-15 minutes

Perhaps God is offering you an invitation to enlarge your understanding or to do something in the next few days. What might that be? Sit quietly for a few minutes, pondering this question: *What do I need to know from this passage?*

❶ Read the instructions above out loud and repeat the question printed in italics. Ask group members to respond by saying, "I sense this passage calling me to . . . ." Then complete that statement with a short phrase. Anyone who wishes to pass may do so.

Praying   5-10 minutes

Take a few minutes to respond to God about this meditation. How do you feel about what you sensed (or didn't sense)? What is it you most want to say to God at this time?

❶ After allowing a few minutes for private prayer, ask group members to pray for the person on their left. Anyone wishing to pray silently may do so by saying, "I'm praying silently," and signifying when he or she is finished by saying "Amen."

Daily Lectio

If you wish, use the above format to meditate on God's Word between group meetings. You may want to focus on today's passage every day this week, or you can use the following passages:

- Psalm 103:11-14 (the greatness of the Father's love)
- Isaiah 62:1-5 (God's delight in His people)
- Luke 15:1-7 (for review: the parable of the lost sheep)
- Luke 15:25-32 (how the father handled the elder son's resentment)
- John 14:23 (how God makes His home within us)
- 1 John 4:15-17 (how we can rely on the Father's love)

---

1. J. A. Thompson, *Handbook of Life in Bible Times* (Downers Grove, Ill.: InterVarsity Press, 1986), p. 105.

Depending on God to Love Me

Psalm 18:4-19

❶ After group members have had a chance to greet each other, lead them through the warming up instructions and then present the question, letting them reflect quietly for a few minutes. Repeat the question and ask group members to share their thoughts in a sentence or two. Anyone who wishes to pass may do so.

Warming Up   5-10 minutes
Close your eyes and sit in the quiet. Relax yourself by breathing in and out several times. Loosen up each muscle one by one as you let go of the things that distract you. When you're ready, consider this quiet question to help focus your thoughts for meditation. Let's say that someone delights in you. What color does that bring to mind?

Reading the Passage   15-20 minutes
Read the following passage. For now, ignore the underlined and italicized words, and the words listed in the shaded box.

❶ Ask a group member to read the passage aloud. Suggest that other group members close their eyes as they listen.

Psalm 18:4-19

DEEP TROUBLE
⁴The *cords of death* entangled me;
    the torrents of destruction overwhelmed me.

⁵The cords of the grave coiled around me;
   the snares of death confronted me.
⁶In my distress I called to the LORD;
   I cried to my God for help.

GOD HEARS

From his *temple* he heard my voice;
   my cry came before him, into his ears.
⁷The *earth trembled* and quaked,
      and the foundations of the mountains shook;
      they trembled because he was angry.
⁸*Smoke* rose from his nostrils;
      consuming fire came from his mouth,
      burning coals blazed out of it.

GOD RESCUES

⁹He parted the *heavens* and came down;
      dark clouds were under his feet.
¹⁰He mounted the *cherubim* and flew;
      he soared on the *wings of the wind.*
¹¹He made *darkness his covering, his canopy* around him—
   the dark rain clouds of the sky.
¹²Out of the brightness of his presence clouds advanced,
   with *hailstones* and *bolts of lightning.*
¹³The LORD thundered from heaven;
   the voice of the Most High resounded.
¹⁴He shot his *arrows* and scattered the enemies,
   great bolts of lightning and routed them.
¹⁵The *valleys of the sea* were exposed
   and the foundations of the earth laid bare
at your rebuke, O LORD,
   at the blast of *breath from your nostrils.*
¹⁶He reached down from on high and took hold of me;
   he drew me out of *deep waters.*

Here are some props and scenery to help you imagine this psalm:

cords of death	wings of the wind
temple	canopy of darkness
trembling earth	hailstones
smoke	lightning bolts
consuming fire	arrows
burning coals	valleys of the sea (ocean floor)
heavens	God's breath
dark clouds	deep waters
cherubim	

SUMMARY

¹⁷He rescued me from my powerful enemy,
   from my foes, who were too strong for me.
¹⁸They confronted me in the day of my disaster,
   but the LORD was my support.
¹⁹He brought me out into a spacious place;
   he rescued me because he delighted in me.

Take a minute to consider the following questions.

❶ Ask group members to look at the questions below. After a few minutes, have them choose one question and share their answer in a sentence or two. Remind them that this is not a time for discussion but for reporting responses to the questions.

David's Experiences

1. This psalm might seem melodramatic, but verse 1 says David sang this to the Lord "when the LORD delivered him from the hand of all his enemies and from the hand of Saul." Read the following background facts about David fleeing Saul, and write down three words that describe how you would have felt if you were David.

   ■ Saul repeatedly tried to kill David, even though David was his son-in-law, the best friend of his son, and the captain of his bodyguard. (1 Samuel 22:14)
   ■ To escape from Saul, David fled to the desert, lived in caves, and stayed with foreign kings.
   ■ The first time Saul tried to kill David, David was playing the harp to soothe him, and Saul hurled a spear at him. (1 Samuel 18:10-11)
   ■ One time David had to escape from Saul through a window.
     (1 Samuel 19:11-12)
   ■ In another desperate attempt to escape from Saul, David stayed with Achish king of Gath where he had to pretend to be insane in order to ensure his safety. To keep up the game, he made marks on the doors of the gate and let saliva run down his beard. (1 Samuel 21:10-15)
   ■ When Ahimelech the priest inquired of the Lord for David, Saul had him killed as well as eighty-five other priests. (1 Samuel 22:9-18)
   ■ After David saved the city of Keilah, he had to flee because the people of Keilah were going to surrender him to Saul. (1 Samuel 23:5-12)
   ■ David spared Saul's life several times. (1 Samuel 24:1-15)

2. David summarized his rescue by saying God "brought me out into a spacious place" (Psalm 18:19). Think about the word *spacious* — enough space to do what? To think what? To feel what? To be what?

3. David went on to say that God rescued him "because he delighted in me" (verse 19). Have you ever felt that God delighted in you? If so, when? If not, what would a person have to do to get God to delight in him?

Picturing the Passage   10-15 minutes
Before reading the passage again, consider these cues.

Cultural Cue: Saul's Spear
At least three times, David narrowly escaped being killed by Saul's spear (1 Samuel 18:10-11, 19:9-10, 20:33). This terrifying weapon probably had a long wooden shaft and was as tall as Saul, who was a head taller than most people (1 Samuel 9:2). Spearheads in those days were made of stone or metal, and the tip often had two hooks or barbs, which left a mortal wound when the spear was pulled out. (The spearhead of Goliath weighed over fifteen pounds!) Some spears were designed to spin through the air, inflicting even greater injury.[1] Take a moment to picture a spear like Saul's in your mind. Let yourself imagine what it would be like to have a large man threaten you with such a weapon.

Setting Cue
If a movie were made of this passage, a props coordinator and director would have certain responsibilities. The shaded box on page 38 contains a list of the items and special effects a props coordinator would need to come up with. Read the list slowly, underline the words you think relate to God's majesty, and circle the ones related to God's effort to rescue the psalmist.

❶ Read the above cues and ask group members to look over the list in the shaded box.

The director of this movie would have to pay attention to action—what the characters do. Underline the action words (verbs) in verses 9-19. The first few action words have been underlined for you. As you continue to underline, notice how the words relate to God's majesty as well as God's rescue of David.

Now you're ready to read the passage aloud. As you do so, picture the events as they happen and picture yourself as the one being rescued. Imagine the items listed as props and the activities the "director" would have orchestrated.

❶ Ask a group member to read the passage aloud as the other members picture the events, complete with props and direction.

Soaking In the Passage   5-15 minutes

Consider how this passage touches your life today. Read the passage aloud again
and ponder the following question for several minutes: *What dramatic moment,
image, sight, or sound emerges from the passage and stays with you?*

After a few minutes, write about the scene or image that resonates within you
from the passage.

I hear . . . I see . . .

❶ Ask a group member to read the passage aloud and then state the question printed in
italics. After some inward reflection, have each member fill in the blank. Ask group
members to read what they've written. Anyone who wishes to pass may do so.

Pondering the Invitation   5-15 minutes

This passage invites you to ponder the great extent to which our majestic God
delights in you. *How do you respond to the idea that God delights in you?* Ponder
this by saying to God, "Show me what I need to know to understand more fully
how You delight in me."

❶ Read the above instructions aloud and repeat the question printed in italics. After a
few minutes, ask group members to respond by saying, "I sense this passage calling
me to. . . ." Then complete that statement with a short phrase. Anyone who wishes
to pass may do so.

Praying   5-10 minutes

Take a few minutes to respond to God about this Scripture passage. How do you
feel about what you sensed (or didn't sense)? What would you like to say to God at
this time?

❶ After allowing a few minutes for private prayer, ask group members to pray for the
person on their left. Anyone wishing to pray silently may do so by saying, "I'm
praying silently," and signifying when he or she is finished by saying "Amen."

Daily Lectio

If you wish, use the above format to meditate on God's Word between group meetings. You may wish to focus on today's passage every day this week, or you can
use the following passages:

- Psalm 22:1-8 (God delights in those He delivers)
- Psalm 37:23-24 (when God delights in someone, He makes his or her steps
  firm)

- Psalm 147:5-11 (God delights in those who hope in His unfailing love)
- Psalm 149:1-4 (God delights in our praise)
- Zephaniah 3:17 (God rejoices over us with singing)
- Matthew 12:18-21 (God delights in Jesus)

---

1. V. Gilbert Beers, *The Victor Journey Through the Bible* (Wheaton, Ill.: Victor Books, 1986), p. 111.

God Cares for My Needs
1 Kings 19:3-13,15-16

❶ After group members have had a chance to greet each other, read the warming up instructions. Then present the quiet question and let group members reflect on it for a few minutes. Repeat the question and ask them to share their thoughts in a sentence or two. Anyone who wishes to pass may do so.

Warming Up   5-10 minutes

Center yourself by breathing in and out several times. Relax your neck and then take time to let your muscles go limp. Offer your distracting thoughts to God, one by one. Then ask yourself the following quiet question to help focus your thoughts for meditation on today's passage: What kinds of experiences make me feel like saying, "I've had enough, Lord"? Close your eyes and take a few minutes to consider the events and the people in your life.

Reading the Passage   15-20 minutes

Read silently the Scripture passage below, noting the explanations in the shaded boxes on pages 44-45.

❶ Ask a group member to read the Scripture passage aloud. Suggest that other group members close their eyes as they listen.

1 Kings 19:3-13,15-16

DESPAIR

³Elijah was *afraid* and ran for his life. When he came to Beersheba in Judah, he left his servant there, ⁴while he himself went a day's journey into the desert. He came to a broom tree, sat down under it and prayed that he might die. "I have had enough, LORD," he said. "Take my life; I am no better than my ancestors."

TENDER MERCIES

⁵Then he lay down under the tree and fell asleep.

All at once an angel touched him and said, "Get up and eat." ⁶He looked around, and there by his head was a cake of *bread* baked over hot coals, and a jar of water. He ate and drank and then lay down again.

⁷The angel of the LORD came back a second time and touched him and said, "Get up and eat, for the journey is too much for you." ⁸So he got up and ate and drank. Strengthened by that food, he *traveled forty days* and forty nights until he reached *Horeb,* the mountain of God. ⁹There he went into a cave and spent the night.

CONVERSATION WITH THE ALMIGHTY

And the word of the LORD came to him: "What are you doing here, Elijah?"

¹⁰He replied, "I have been very zealous for the LORD God Almighty. The Israelites have rejected your covenant, broken down your altars, and put your prophets to death with the sword. I am the *only one left,* and now they are trying to kill me too."

¹¹The LORD said, "Go out and stand on the mountain in the presence of the LORD, for the LORD is about to pass by."

Afraid — Ahab and Jezebel, monarchs of Israel, worshiped Baal, a foreign god that Elijah prophesied against. Elijah challenged the prophets of Baal to a contest in which Elijah proved God's power by calling down fire from heaven on his sacrifice. Baal's prophets got no response for their sacrifice and "lost" the contest.

Bread — Loaves of bread were flat, like extra-thick pancakes.

Traveled forty days — Elijah ran the length of Israel from north to south (ninety miles). From there he ran to Mt. Horeb in the southern tip of Arabia (two hundred to three hundred miles, depending on the route).[1]

Horeb — Another name for Mt. Sinai, where God conversed with Moses centuries earlier.

Only one left — Jezebel had ordered the death of all the Lord's prophets (18:4).

Then a great and powerful wind tore the mountains apart and shattered the rocks before the LORD, but the LORD was not in the wind. After the wind there was an earthquake, but the LORD was not in the earthquake. [12]After the earthquake came a fire, but the LORD was not in the fire. And after the fire came a gentle whisper. [13]When Elijah heard it, he pulled his cloak over his face and went out and stood at the mouth of the cave. . . .

[15]The LORD said to him, "Go back the way you came, and . . . anoint Hazael king over Aram. [16]. . . anoint Jehu son of Nimshi king over Israel, and anoint Elisha son of Shaphat from Abel Meholah to succeed you as prophet.

If you haven't read the notes in the shaded boxes, read them silently now. Take a minute to consider the following questions.

➊ After someone reads the Scripture passage, ask group members to read the explanations in the shaded boxes and then jot down answers to the questions below. After a few minutes, have them choose one question and share their answer in a sentence or two. Anyone who wishes to pass may do so. Explain that this is not a time for discussion but for reporting responses to the questions.

God's Interaction with Elijah

1. It's difficult to understand how Elijah could be so intimidated by Jezebel after he'd just won the tremendous victory over the prophets of Baal. Can you think of other reasons he felt down?

   ■ "Emotional highs" (such as defeating the prophets of Baal) can beget "emotional lows."
   ■ He felt alone without the other prophets of God.
   ■ This was the last straw.
   ■ He had thought Ahab and Jezebel would give in, but they didn't.
   ■
   ■

2. Bible accounts get softened and sanitized in the frequency of telling. Consider how you would respond to the following experiences and put yourself in Elijah's place. Rank these experiences from 1-4, giving a 1 to the experience that would have been the most emotionally draining for you.

Anoint—To set aside for a special purpose; one of the many prophetic duties, besides standing up to the wicked and preaching God's messages.

Elisha—This man went on to become Elijah's famous protégé who performed many miracles and managed to see God's chariots of fire coming to help when no one else could (2 Kings 6:17).

___ receiving a death threat
___ feeling suicidal
___ making a long journey on foot
___ encountering an angel

3. Which of the details about the angel's service to Elijah is most meaningful to you?

☐ The angel respected Elijah's need for rest and made it possible.
☐ The angel provided what appears to have been a prepared meal ("cake of bread baked over hot coals").
☐ The meal the angel provided was substantial enough to sustain Elijah for forty days.
☐ The simplicity of the angel's provision: a few words and simple but substantial food.

4. Although God knew about Elijah's troubles, he still asked, "What are you doing here, Elijah?" Why do you think God might have done that?

☐ Talking directly to God is important.
☐ Talking helps clarify problems.
☐ Talking provides relief.
☐ other:

5. Elijah was experienced enough in the ways of God to recognize God's voice in the gentle whisper instead of looking to the rock-shattering wind, earthquake, or fire. Write a couple of sentences to God about your ability (or lack of ability) to recognize God's gentle whisper and what you desire to happen in this matter.

6. Part of how God responded to the discouraged prophet, Elijah, was to give him more work to do, including the anointing of a successor, Elisha. Elijah and Elisha bonded to the point that it seems likely that Elijah never again felt he was the "only one left." Has there been a time when you felt lonely, but God provided you with unexpected sources of joy and companionship? If so, when?

Picturing the Passage
10–15 minutes

Before reading the passage again, consider this cue.

Setting Cue: Elijah Under the Tree

Picture Elijah, who'd had it, sitting in the desert under a broom tree—a large shrub which can grow up to thirteen feet high.[2] Elijah was known for wearing a garment made of haircloth and a girdle (wide belt), and he had just made a two-hundred-mile journey to Mount Horeb across wild, barren wilderness (2 Kings 1:8).

Now read the passage again—aloud this time—and picture these scenes:

- Elijah sitting under the tree
- God providing Elijah tender mercies: sleep, food, and sympathy
- Elijah running off to an even more remote place to seek God
- Elijah watching the great and powerful wind tearing the mountains apart and shattering the rocks; feeling the earthquake; seeing the fire; and finally hearing the gentle whisper

> ❶ Have group members read this cue silently. Then ask a group member to read the passage aloud while the others picture it.

Soaking In the Passage
5–15 minutes

Think about how this passage touches you by reading the passage aloud and pondering this question: *What dramatic moment, scene, or sound emerges from the passage and stays with me?* If you latch on to something right away, set that aside for a minute and see if anything else emerges.

After a few minutes, write about the moment, scene, or sound that resonates within you from the passage.

I hear . . . I see . . .

> ❶ Ask a group member to read the passage aloud and then state the question printed in italics. After some inward reflection, have each member fill in the blank. Ask group members to read what they've written. Anyone who wishes to pass may do so.

Pondering the Invitation
5–15 minutes

God knows our needs for purpose and for physical and emotional renewal. He is eager to meet those needs. Perhaps God is inviting you to let Him meet needs you have never laid before Him to any degree. Sit quietly for a few minutes, pondering this question: *What needs do I sense God asking me to surrender?* If nothing comes to mind, simply enjoy resting in God, who supplies all our needs.

❶ Read the above instructions aloud and repeat the question printed in italics. After a few minutes, ask group members to respond by completing the statement, "I sense this passage calling me to. . . ." Then complete that statement with a short phrase. Anyone who wishes to pass may do so.

Praying   5-10 minutes
Take a few minutes to respond to God about this meditation time. How do you feel about what you sensed (or didn't sense) God saying to you? What is it you most want to say to God at this time?

❶ After allowing a few minutes for private prayer, ask group members to pray for the person on their left. Anyone wishing to pray silently may do so by saying, "I'm praying silently," then signifying when he or she is finished by saying "Amen."

Daily Lectio
If you wish, use the above format to meditate on God's Word between group meetings. You may wish to focus on today's passage every day this week, or you can use the following passages:

- Psalm 61:1-6 (God, our rock and refuge)
- Psalm 91:1-6 (God, our protection from terror)
- Psalm 116:1-7 (how God gives rest when we're in great need)
- Psalm 147:1-7 (how God heals the brokenhearted)
- 2 Corinthians 9:6-8 (God provides everything we need)
- Philippians 4:19 (God meets all our needs)

---

1. D. Guthrie and J. A. Motyer, *The New Bible Commentary* (Grand Rapids, Mich.: Eerdmans, 1991), p. 345.
2. J. A. Thompson, *Handbook of Life in Bible Times* (Downers Grove, Ill.: InterVarsity Press, 1986), p. 22.

Part Two

MAKING PROGRESS
IN THE SPIRITUAL LIFE

When You Want to Let God Change You

Getting Involved in the Text

Why so much emphasis on beginning each session by deep breathing?

We spend all day responding to stimuli—answering the telephone, following schedules, evaluating what needs to be done next. When we're finally quiet, these activities remain "traffic in our heads" that keeps us from focusing on God. One way to interrupt this traffic is to focus on being present in the moment by breathing in and out deeply, even overdoing it. It is also helpful to relax parts of your body one by one: bending your neck, letting your arms go limp, relaxing your legs and ankles. Loosen each part from the inside out. These exercises do not mean that you're setting aside your mind; you're simply redirecting it away from the busyness of the day to prepare yourself to wait on the still, small voice of God.

In the meditation section (Picturing the Passage), imagine the setting, but don't try too hard to create a careful, detailed picture. Your goal is to let God speak to you, not to imagine a perfect reconstruction of the event. The Cultural Cues will help you immerse yourself in the passage and set aside distractions. They ground you in a concrete way—What am I seeing or smelling?—but don't get obsessed with them. Establish yourself in the setting and then move through the passage to let God speak to you.

Sometimes the whole scene will elude you, but a particular word or image will stand out. Once when I reflected on the woman with the issue of blood, I was struck by the words "whole truth" which she told Jesus. I felt her embarrassment as she spoke out. I saw her made publicly vulnerable to Jesus, the Prophet, and it made me see just how real I could be with God.

God Enlarges My Understanding
John 3:1-17

❶ After your group has had a chance to greet each other, read the bulleted instructions, then ask the quiet question. Sit together for a couple of minutes, then repeat the question. Ask group members to share their thoughts in a sentence or two. Anyone who wishes to pass may do so. After group members share, thank them and comment that it's helpful to hear the variety of ways God speaks to people.

Warming Up   5-10 minutes
Begin each session by quieting yourself in silence. These habits may help:

- Breathe in and out deeply five or six times. Relax your neck and move it around. Then let your arms go limp and relax the legs and ankles. Relax each part from the inside out.
- Use the "palms down, palms up" method to turn your distractions over to God. Rest your hands in your lap, placing the palms down whenever you think of concerns you need to turn over to God. Turn your palms up as a symbol of your desire to receive from the Lord and set aside distractions.

Ask yourself the following quiet question to focus your thoughts for the meditation: What draws you to a group/individual study like this? Close your eyes and reflect on your past experiences or pressing needs in your life. It's okay if nothing comes to mind right away. If so, simply enjoy resting in God's presence.

Reading the Passage   5-10 minutes
If you have read about Nicodemus before, set aside what you've heard about him or the central idea of the passage. Read the passage silently, trying to hear it as if you've never heard it before. Note the explanations in the shaded boxes at the bottoms of pages 52-53 as you read along, or read them afterward.

❶ Ask a group member to read the passage below aloud. Suggest that other group members close their eyes as they listen.

John 3:1-17

¹Now there was a man of the *Pharisees* named Nicodemus, a member of the *Jewish ruling council.*

NICODEMUS ADMITS JESUS IS ONTO SOMETHING

²He came to Jesus at night and said, "Rabbi, we know you are a teacher who has come from God. For no one could perform the miraculous signs you are doing if God were not with him."

³In reply Jesus declared, "I tell you the truth, no one can see the kingdom of God unless he is born again."

NICODEMUS ASKS QUESTIONS

⁴"How can a man be born when he is old?" Nicodemus asked. "Surely he cannot enter a second time into his mother's womb to be born!"

⁵Jesus answered, "I tell you the truth, no one can enter the *kingdom of God* unless he is *born of water* and the Spirit. ⁶Flesh gives birth to flesh, but the Spirit gives birth to spirit. ⁷You should not be surprised at my saying, 'You must be born again.' ⁸The wind blows wherever it pleases. You hear its sound, but you cannot tell where it comes from or where it is going. So it is with everyone *born of the Spirit.*"

⁹"How can this be?" Nicodemus asked.

JESUS EXPLAINS ETERNAL LIFE

¹⁰"You are Israel's teacher," said Jesus, "and do you not understand these things? . . . ¹³No one has ever gone into heaven except the one who came from heaven—the *Son of Man.* ¹⁴*Just as Moses* lifted up the snake in the desert, so the Son of Man must be lifted up, ¹⁵that

---

Pharisees—This powerful group of religious experts was created to reform society from its wrongs. They considered certain traditions to be equally authoritative with the Law, and they sometimes overemphasized these traditions. Later in Jesus' ministry, He criticized them harshly (Matthew 23).

Jewish ruling council—This probably refers to the Sanhedrin, a council of seventy elders who ruled the Jewish people. As a whole, this council hated Jesus and considered Him an impostor.

Kingdom of God—God's rule on earth, beginning with Jesus' coming, continuing through the present and into the future.

Born of water—This could refer to physical childbirth ("breaking of water") or Christian baptism, or perhaps both.   *continued*

everyone who believes in him may have eternal life.
[16]"For God so loved the world that he gave his one and only Son, that whoever believes in him shall not perish but have eternal life. [17]For God did not send his Son into the world to condemn the world, but to save the world through him."

If you haven't read the notes in the shaded boxes, read them now. Take a minute to consider the following questions.

---

❶ After the passage is read, ask group members to read the explanations in the shaded boxes and then jot down answers to the questions below. After a few minutes, have them choose one question and share their answer in a sentence or two. Anyone who wishes to pass may do so. Explain that this is not a time for discussion but for reporting responses to the questions.

Nicodemus

1. How would you describe Nicodemus, based on these actions:

Even though Nicodemus was a Jewish leader, he was willing to go outside established opinion and to approach Jesus with several "how can this be?" questions (verses 4,9).

☐ curious
☐ truth-seeker
☐ bold enough to ask
☐ testing Jesus
☐ belligerent
☐ persistent
☐ other:

Nicodemus responded to Jesus' statements with more questions and confusion. Why do you think he did that? Because he was . . .

☐ humble
☐ obtuse
☐ literal-minded
☐ appalled
☐ trying to misunderstand
☐ other:

Born of . . . the Spirit—This could refer to a beginning of spiritual awareness or to a continual awakening to God.

Son of Man—A phrase from the Old Testament that Jesus used to describe Himself as the Messiah promised by Daniel (Daniel 7:13).

Just as Moses—Centuries earlier, poisonous snakes infested the Israelite camp. People were saved by looking at a bronze snake that Moses lifted up (Numbers 21:8-9).

Jesus

2. What do you learn about Jesus from His willingness to talk to Nicodemus?

☐ approachable, ready to be asked questions
☐ available for one-on-one conversation
☐ not easily intimidated by authority
☐ other:

3. What were Jesus' expectations, perhaps frustrations, expressed in this phrase: "You are Israel's teacher," said Jesus, "and do you not understand these things?" (verse 10).

☐ unimpressed with the scholarship of the Pharisees
☐ unimpressed by the Pharisees' grasp of spiritual issues
☐ expecting Nicodemus to understand too much
☐ challenging Nicodemus to dig deeper
☐ other:

Symbols

4. Which of the following images that Jesus used is most helpful to you? Put a check mark by that one.

☐ birth to illustrate how spiritual transformation occurs
☐ wind to illustrate how the Spirit moves in the world
☐ raising the bronze snake to symbolize how the Son of Man must be lifted up, and that everyone who believes in Him as Messiah may have eternal life

Which image, if any, invites you to ponder it more fully? Put a question mark by that one.

If any of the above questions are too difficult, hold them before God for a few minutes and then go on. Don't worry about getting an answer, but be open to what may come to you in the next few days.

Picturing the Passage   10–15 minutes
Before reading the passage again, consider these cues. Let them help you picture how this event in Scripture might have occurred.

Character Cue: Nicodemus, the Pharisee
Even though Nicodemus was a Pharisee (the political party of reformers and good-deed doers), he was also humble and sensitive to truth. This event occurred early in Jesus' three-year ministry, and so Nicodemus may not have witnessed any of Jesus' miracles. He may have been confused about who Jesus was, yet his confusion did not lead him to name-calling and faulty generalizations. It led him to seek Jesus.

Character Cue: Jesus, the Enemy of the Pharisees

Jesus later accused the Pharisees of hypocrisy (doing great deeds but overlooking the inner person), but He didn't level such a charge at Nicodemus. Jesus did, however, question Nicodemus and stretch him, as He did with His disciples and does with people today.

Setting Cue: Where Did They Talk?

Nicodemus came to see Jesus at night, presumably because he didn't want to be seen by other leaders. His intense discussion with Jesus appears to have been private and may have taken place by lamplight or perhaps in the night air. Several paintings show them talking on a flat rooftop—a logical place to meet at night. There was often an upper room built on the flat roof where they may have also met in private.

Now read the passage aloud and picture the events as if they were a movie playing in your mind. For example, imagine two robed men sitting on stools on an open rooftop. They lean close together in order to speak softly. The night sky is velvet black, glittering with stars because there are no city lights to obscure them. Smell the scent of lamp oil, and feel the light breeze that makes the lamplight flicker.

Or, imagine the moistness of an evening walk. Perhaps Nicodemus became anxious for sunset on this spring evening, knowing what he had in mind.

> ❶ Have group members read the above cues. Then have a group member read the passage aloud while the others picture the passage.

Soaking In the Passage   5-15 minutes

Consider this all-important question whenever you read Scripture: How is my life touched today by this passage?

Read the passage aloud again and ponder the following question for about five minutes: *What word, phrase, scene, or image emerges from the passage and stays with me?* If you latch on to something right away, set that aside for a minute and see if anything else emerges.

Here are some examples of phrases, scenes, or images:

- hearing the wind blow as Jesus talked about the Spirit
- Nicodemus's desire to understand when he asked, "How can this be?" (verse 9)
- phrases (circle one): kingdom of God, Spirit gives birth to spirit, lifted up

After a few minutes, write about the word, phrase, scene, or image that resonates within you from the passage.

Word or phrase:

Scene or image:

I hear . . . I see . . .

> ❶ Have a different group member read the passage aloud and then state the question printed in italics. Have the group sit together quietly and then write down the word or image that comes to mind. After a few minutes, ask each group member to read what they've written. Anyone who wishes to pass may do so.

Pondering the Invitation   5-15 minutes
Perhaps God is offering you an invitation of some kind through this passage—something you need to do within the next day or two. What might that be? Sit quietly for a few minutes, pondering this question: *What do I sense this passage calling me to do or be?* If nothing comes, that's fine. Watch for insights in the next few days, but for now, simply sit in the quiet and enjoy God's presence.

> ❶ Read the above instructions aloud. After a few minutes, repeat the question printed in italics. Ask group members to respond by saying, "I sense this passage calling me to. . . ." Then complete that statement with a short phrase. Anyone who wishes to pass may do so. Encourage group members to listen respectfully and prayerfully to other members.

Praying   5-10 minutes
Take a few minutes to respond to God about this meditation. How do you feel about what you sensed (or didn't sense)? What do you most want to say to God at this time?

> ❶ After allowing a few minutes for private prayer, ask group members to pray for the person on their left. Anyone wishing to pray silently may do so by saying, "I'm praying silently," then signifying when he or she is finished by saying "Amen."

Daily Lectio
If you wish, use the above format to meditate on God's Word between group meetings. You may wish to focus on today's passage every day this week (try using a different version of the Bible besides NIV) or use the following passages:

   ■ Deuteronomy 4:29 (finding God when you look for Him with all your heart and soul)

- John 12:24-26 (dying to self)
- Romans 12:2 (being transformed)
- 1 Corinthians 15:45-50 (the necessity of being born again)
- 2 Corinthians 4:16-18 (focusing on the unseen)
- 1 Peter 1:20-23 (the difference being born again makes)

Drawn into Deeper Obedience
Luke 13:22-30

❶ After group members have had a chance to greet each other, read the centering instructions. Then present the quiet question and let them reflect silently for a few minutes. Repeat the question and ask them to share their thoughts in a sentence or two. Anyone who wishes to pass may do so.

Warming Up   5-10 minutes

Center yourself by breathing in and out slowly several times. Relax your neck and then take time to relax the rest of your body. Set aside each distraction as it comes to your mind. Close your eyes and put yourself in the place of the writer of Psalm 23. You now sit at "a table before me in the presence of my enemies." Those "enemies" might be hurry, fatigue, or deadlines, but you have these few minutes to sit at a table with Jesus, disregard those enemies, and enjoy the quiet with Jesus.

As you sit in the quiet, consider this question: What progress in the spiritual life has God brought about in me recently? If an answer to the above question doesn't come to you right away, that's fine. Try to enjoy God's presence without having to do anything.

Reading the Passage   15-20 minutes

Read the Scripture passage printed below, noting the explanations in the shaded box on page 60.

❶ Ask a group member to read the Scripture passage aloud. Suggest that other group members close their eyes as they listen.

Luke 13:22-30

CHALLENGING CIRCUMSTANCES

²²Then Jesus went through the towns and villages, teaching as he *made his way to Jerusalem.*

CHALLENGING TALK

²³Someone asked him, "Lord, are only a few people going to *be saved?*"

He said to them, ²⁴"Make every effort to enter through the *narrow door,* because many, I tell you, will try to enter and will not be able to. ²⁵Once the owner of the house gets up and closes the door, you will stand outside knocking and pleading, 'Sir, open the door for us.'

"But he will answer, 'I don't know you or where you come from.'

²⁶"Then you will say, 'We ate and drank with you, and you taught in our streets.'

²⁷"But he will reply, 'I don't know you or where you come from. Away from me, all you evildoers!'

²⁸"There will be weeping there, and *gnashing of teeth,* when you see Abraham, Isaac and Jacob and all the prophets in the kingdom of God, but you yourselves thrown out."

SHOCKING RESULTS

²⁹People will come from *east and west and north and south,* and will take their places at the feast in the kingdom of God. ³⁰Indeed there are *those who are last who will be first,* and first who will be last."

If you haven't read the notes in the shaded box, read them now. Take a minute to consider the following questions.

Made his way to Jerusalem — Jesus knew that He would die in Jerusalem and had told His disciples (Luke 9:43-45,51).

Be saved — The accepted answer to this question was that all Jews, except heretics and gross sinners, would enter the kingdom. Jesus refused to speculate and instead spoke directly to the person asking the question.

Narrow door — This symbolizes the challenge of the kingdom life — to die to self and live to God. Most people choose the wide gate, but this unpopular narrow door "leads to life" (Matthew 7:13).

Gnashing of teeth — Grinding teeth in anguish.

East and west and north and south — This largely Jewish audience may have been shocked that the kingdom would include so many outside their world.

Those who are last will be first — Popularity, status, wealth, and power are of little value to the kingdom. Knowing Christ is what matters (verse 25).

❶ After the passage is read, ask group members to read the explanations in the shaded box and then jot down answers to the questions below. After a few minutes, have them choose one question and share their answer in a sentence or two. Anyone who wishes to pass may do so. Explain that this is not a time for discussion but for reporting responses to the questions.

Challenging Circumstances

1. Jesus was on His way to His own murder. Which of the following phrases seems especially meaningful to you in light of that fact?

   ☐ Many, I tell you, will try to enter and will not be able to.
   ☐ When you see Abraham, Isaac, and Jacob, and all the prophets in the kingdom of God.
   ☐ Make every effort to enter through the narrow door.
   ☐ Those who are last who will be first.
   ☐ other:

Why does the phrase you picked seem most meaningful?

Challenging Talk

2. If you had been a good Jew living in that day, who assumed that "the saved" would consist of other good Jews like yourself, what statements of Jesus would have shocked you? Underline them in the text.

3. In what area of your life has God been challenging you recently to enter by the "narrow door," even if it means being "last," according to someone else's standards?

   ☐ having integrity at work
   ☐ treating people with kindness
   ☐ showing compassion for the throwaways of society
   ☐ wanting to forgive others
   ☐ other (choose something related to love, joy, peace, patience, kindness, goodness, faithfulness, gentleness, and self-control):

Shocking Results

4. How do these shocking results affect you? Check the appropriate box.

   ■ People whom I think of as outsiders will come to the feast.

      ☐ displeased   ☐ pleased   ☐ no response

   ■ The things I struggle to acquire now will not matter.

      ☐ displeased   ☐ pleased   ☐ no response

Picturing the Passage   10-15 minutes

Before reading the passage again, consider these cues.

Character Cue: Jesus Focused on the Questioner, Not the Question

What was behind the question "someone" asked Jesus, "Lord, are only a few people going to be saved (verse 23)?" Did this person ask out of a sincere desire to know, or because it was (and is) a problematic question and he figured this new prophet, Jesus, might have an interesting answer? In either case, Jesus set aside the hypothetical nature of the question and spoke directly to the questioner, "You there, you questioner, make every effort to enter through the narrow door. . . ." Jesus cared more about the individual questioning Him than answering a lofty religious query.

Character Cue: Jesus Taught with Paradoxes

Jesus painted pictures that make us wonder, *How can this be?* In this passage, He painted a picture of people converging from the east and west and north and south on a narrow door and walking through it. This picture was inclusive (from all nations) but exclusive (many would be excluded).

Now that you've considered these cues, read the passage aloud and then close your eyes, picturing one of these scenes:

- the narrow door and what it would take to walk through it
- the narrow door with thousands of people different from you passing through it
- you, as the questioner, being told by the Great Teacher to make every effort to enter through the narrow door;
- a picture of your own:

> ❶ Have group members read the cue silently. Then have a group member read the passage aloud while the others picture the passage.

Soaking In the Passage   5-10 minutes

Consider how your life is touched today by this passage. Read the passage aloud again and ponder the following question for a few minutes: *Find within this passage a word or phrase that resonates with you.* If you latch on to something right away, set that aside for a minute and see if anything else emerges. After a few minutes, write about the word or phrase that seems to speak to you.

Word or phrase:

🄛 Have a different group member read the passage aloud and then state the question printed in italics. Have the group sit quietly for a minute and then write the word or phrase that comes to mind. Then ask group members to read what they've written. Anyone who wishes to pass may do so.

Pondering the Invitation

Perhaps God is offering you an invitation in this passage to be challenged in some way. If so, don't feel you're being preached at. Jesus said to make every effort to enter the narrow door, even as He was aware of the narrowest of doors that awaited Him—His own murder. He knew the difficulty of the kingdom's "narrow door." Sit quietly for a few minutes, pondering these two questions:

■ *What are the "narrow doors" in my life?*
■ *Why is it important for Jesus to know me and where I come from (verse 25) in order for me to pass through that "narrow door"?*

You may wish to use the blank space on the following page to write your answer.

🄛 Read the above instructions aloud. After a few minutes, repeat the questions printed in italics and ask group members to respond by saying, "I sense this passage calling me to. . . ." Then complete that statement with a short phrase. Anyone who wishes to pass may do so.

Praying

Take a few minutes to respond to God about this "narrow door."

🄛 After allowing a few minutes for private prayer, ask group members to pray for the person on their left, according to what that person said in "Pondering the Invitation." Anyone wishing to pray silently may do so by saying, "I'm praying silently," then signifying when he or she is finished by saying "Amen."

Daily Lectio

If you wish, use the above format to meditate on God's Word between group meetings. You may wish to focus on today's passage every day this week, or you can use the following passages:

■ Matthew 7:13-20 (inward life versus outward appearances, from the parallel passage. A parallel passage is one from another gospel in which the same content is offered from another writer's viewpoint.)
■ Matthew 7:21-23 (more about those who are excluded, from the parallel passage)

- Matthew 7:24-27 (parable of the house built on rock and the one built on sand)
- Ephesians 4:1-6 (humility; making every effort to be a peacemaker)
- Hebrews 12:14-16 (making every effort to be peaceful and holy)
- 2 Peter 1:3-7 (making every effort to progress in faith, goodness, knowledge, self-control, perseverance, godliness, brotherly kindness, and love)

Pursuing God, Not Power

Matthew 20:20-28

● After your group has had a chance to greet one another, ask them to close their eyes, relax their muscles, and breathe deeply. Encourage them to set aside distractions. Read the prayer and the question in the "Warming Up" section. Let them enjoy the silence a few minutes and then ask group members to offer one word regarding themselves as a vessel. After a few more minutes, ask group members to share that word. Anyone who wishes to pass may do so.

Warming Up   5-10 minutes

Sit quietly and breathe in and out several times. Relax your neck and then relax other muscles. If you feel distracted, jot down anything you need to remember and begin turning concerns over to God. Then read the following prayer:

> Use me then, my Savior, for whatever purpose, and in whatever way you may require. Here is my poor heart, an empty vessel; fill it with your grace.[1]
>
> —DWIGHT L. MOODY

Sit for a moment and ponder, What one word describes my self (my "vessel") today?

Reading the Passage   15-20 minutes

If you have read this narrative before, set aside what you know and read the Scripture passage with fresh eyes. As you read, note the explanations in the shaded box.

● Ask a group member to read the passage below aloud. Suggest that other group members close their eyes as they listen.

Matthew 20:20-28

WHAT WE WANT: POWER AND INFLUENCE

²⁰Then the mother of *Zebedee's sons* came to Jesus with her sons and, kneeling down, asked a favor of him.

²¹"What is it you want?" he asked.

She said, "Grant that one of these two sons of mine may *sit at your right and* the other *at your left* in your kingdom."

²²"You don't know what you are asking," Jesus said to them. "Can you drink *the cup* I am going to drink?"

"We can," they answered.

²³Jesus said to them, "You will indeed drink from my cup, but to sit at my right or left is not for me to grant. These places belong to those for whom they have been prepared by my Father."

²⁴When the ten heard about this, they were indignant with the two brothers.

WHAT WE'RE CALLED TO: SERVANTHOOD

²⁵Jesus called them together and said, "You know that the rulers of the Gentiles lord it over them, and their high officials exercise authority over them. ²⁶*Not so with you.* Instead, whoever wants to become great among you must be your servant, ²⁷and whoever wants to be first must be your slave—²⁸just as the Son of Man did not come to be served, but to serve, and to give his life as a ransom for many."

If you haven't read the notes in the shaded box below, read them now. Take a minute to consider the following questions.

---

❶ After the passage is read, ask group members to read the explanations in the shaded box and then jot down answers to the questions that follow. After a few minutes, have them choose one question and share their answer in a sentence or two. Anyone who wishes to pass may do so. Explain that this is not a time for discussion but for reporting responses to the questions.

Zebedee's sons—The apostles James and John, whom Jesus nicknamed "sons of thunder" (Mark 3:17). Later, they would want to call down fire from heaven on Samaritans who wouldn't receive Christ (Luke 9:54).

Sit at your right and at your left—These were positions of power and prestige as Jesus' closest advisors in a supposed earthly kingdom.

The cup—Jesus seems to be referring to His suffering and crucifixion. James was later martyred for His faith and John was exiled.

Not so with you—The cup we take from Jesus—that of being a servant instead of being served—is radically opposed to cultural norms in which self-promotion is not only acceptable but wise. You're considered a fool if you don't serve yourself. But that is not what Jesus asks of us.

Mother of James and John

1. Which of the following reasons might explain why she kneeled? (Mark one or more.)

☐ to worship Christ
☐ to show respect for Christ
☐ to appear worshipful before she asked Christ for what she wanted
☐ other:

The Other Ten Apostles

2. Why do you think they were indignant with James and John? (verse 24)

☐ They were disgusted that the brothers tried to get glory for themselves.
☐ They were disgusted that they didn't think of it first.
☐ Other:

Jesus' Questions

3. Jesus' questions point out opposing forces within our character as Christians.

"What is it you want?"		**"Can you drink the cup I am going to drink?"**
I often want things or power or influence. I often want to do God's will, except that, like James and John's mother, I have specific ideas about what God's will should be.	1. 2. 3.	To drink Christ's cup—to serve instead of being served, to suffer—is unpleasant. It may mean giving up power and influence, as well as my version of God's will.

In the center (above), write down a few issues that bring out this conflict in you, such as relationships, work, or health.

Picturing the Passage

Before reading the passage again, consider these cues.

Character Cue: James and John, the Go-Getters

According to the parallel passage in Mark, the mother of James and John wasn't the only one actively lobbying for them to get high positions. James and John asked for themselves, too: "Teacher," [James and John] said, "we want you to do for us whatever we ask" (Mark 10:35).

On the other hand, their desire for greatness was a common one with which we can identify. They lived in a proud nation, Israel, which had been defeated and dominated by the world's greatest superpower, Rome. In our times, it's not abnormal for a politician to vie for a higher seat in power or an employee to submit a résumé when a higher position opens up. To be fair to James and John, they had left a prosperous fishing company to follow Jesus—a huge step of submission. What would they get for their obedience?

Setting Cue: The Timing of This Discussion

This discussion occurred shortly before Jesus' death. The disciples were on their way to Jerusalem, where Jesus' enemies were looking for Him to kill Him. Because the showdown was imminent, these three may have thought this was their last chance to approach Jesus. Their request created one of many rousing discussions among the disciples, out of which often came a statement from Jesus that was contrary to life but true to God. In their misunderstanding of Jesus, they wanted to honor themselves, while Jesus prepared to humble Himself.

Now that you've looked at these cues, take a few minutes to quiet yourself and then put yourself in the place of James or John or their mother, or one of the other disciples. Picture the scene of James and John's mother kneeling before Jesus, asking for this favor. Picture Jesus' shocking reply that even though Gentile rulers lorded authority over others, it would "not [be] so [among] you." Read the passage—aloud this time—and picture it.

> ❶ Have group members read the above cues silently. Then have a group member read the passage aloud while the others picture the passage.

Soaking In the Passage

Consider now the all-important issue to address whenever you read Scripture—how your life is touched by this passage.

Read the passage aloud again and ponder the following question for a few minutes: *What word, phrase, special moment, or scene emerges from the passage and stays with me?* If you latch on to something right away, set that aside for a minute and see if anything else emerges.

After a few minutes, write about the word, phrase, moment, or scene that resonates within you from the passage.

Word or phrase:

Moment or scene: I hear . . . I see . . .

> ❶ Have a different group member read the passage aloud and then state the question printed in italics. Have the group sit together quietly and then write about the words or scenes that come to mind. After a few minutes, ask group members to read what they've written. Anyone who wishes to pass may do so.

Pondering the Invitation   5-15 minutes

Perhaps God is offering you an invitation in this passage to enlarge your understanding in the next few days. In what way might that be? Sit in the quiet and enjoy it a few minutes, pondering this question: *What do I need to know from this passage?* Be alert, but don't feel pressured to come up with an answer.

> ❶ Read the above instructions aloud. After a few moments, repeat the question printed in italics. Ask group members to respond by saying, "I sense this passage calling me to know. . . ." Then complete that statement with a short phrase. Anyone who wishes to pass may do so.

Praying   5-10 minutes

Take a few minutes to respond to God about what He has shown you: How do you feel about what you sensed (or didn't sense)? What do you want to say to God at this time?

> ❶ After allowing a few minutes for private prayer, ask group members to pray regarding what God has said to them. Anyone wishing to pray silently may do so by saying, "I'm praying silently," then signifying when he or she is finished by saying "Amen."

Daily Lectio

If you wish, use the above format to meditate on God's Word between group meetings. You may wish to focus on today's passage every day this week, or you can use the following passages:

- Galatians 5:13-16 (serving one another in love)
- Philippians 2:1-8 (humbling oneself)
- 1 Peter 5:2-6 (humbling oneself—especially leaders)

- Mark 5:35-43 (Jesus bringing a girl back to life, even when He was laughed at)
- Mark 14:33-41 (Jesus humbling Himself before God in Gethsemane)
- Acts 12:1-2; Revelation 1:1-2,9 (the death of James and the banishment of John, humble servants of God)

---

1. Dwight L. Moody, as quoted in Veronica Zundel, ed., *The Eerdmans Book of Famous Prayers* (Grand Rapids, Mich.: Eerdmans, 1983), p. 81.

Spiritual Realities I Need to See

Ephesians 2:4-10

❶ After group members have had a chance to greet each other, read the centering instructions in the "Warming Up" section. Then present the question and let them reflect quietly for a few minutes. Repeat the question and ask them to share their thoughts in a sentence or two. Anyone who wishes to pass may do so.

Warming Up   5-10 minutes

Center yourself by breathing in and out several times. Relax your legs and arms. Bend your neck back and forth. Let go of distracting thoughts and, if necessary, jot them down to turn them over to God. Then ask yourself the following question to help focus your thoughts for the meditation: In what ways has God worked within me recently?

Close your eyes and take a few minutes to consider the places you've gone and the people you've talked to in the last week. If nothing comes to you, simply enjoy God's presence.

Reading the Passage   15-20 minutes

Read the Scripture passage, noting the explanations in the shaded box below it.

❶ Ask a group member to read the Scripture passage aloud. Suggest that other group members close their eyes as they listen.

Ephesians 2: 4-10

SPIRITUAL AWAKENING

[4]But because of his great love for us, God, who is rich in mercy, [5]*made us alive* with Christ even when we were dead in transgressions — it is by grace you have been saved.

OUR FUTURE

[6]And God raised us up with Christ and seated us with him in the heavenly realms in Christ Jesus, [7]in order that in the coming ages he might show the incomparable riches of his *grace,* expressed in his kindness to us in Christ Jesus.

HOW THIS AWAKENING WORKS

[8]For it is by grace you have been saved, through faith — and this not from yourselves, it is the gift of God — [9]not by works, so that no one can boast. [10]For we are God's workmanship, created in Christ Jesus to do good works, which God prepared in advance for us to do.

If you haven't read the notes in the shaded box, read them now. Take a minute to consider the following questions.

---

❶ After the passage is read, ask group members to read the explanations in the shaded box and then jot down answers to the questions below. After a few minutes, have them choose one question and share their answer in a sentence or two. Anyone who wishes to pass may do so. Explain that this is not a time for discussion but for reporting responses to the questions.

Afterlife Phrases

1. This passage is full of lofty, mysterious phrases that humans would be presumptuous to think they understand. Sure, we can give definitions to certain words, but to say we grasp and understand them is probably not true. Still, we have the capacity to enjoy that which is above our heads.

   Look at the phrases below. Which, if any, make you think, *I'm not sure what it means, but I like the sound of it.*

Made us alive—Awakening from spiritual death. It changes our spiritual status and how we respond to God.

Grace—God's choice to love us when we have done nothing to deserve it.

☐ God . . . his great love for us
☐ incomparable riches of his grace
☐ God . . . rich in mercy
☐ His kindness to us in Christ Jesus
☐ raised us up with Christ
☐ faith . . . the gift of God
☐ seated us with Him in the heavenly realms in Christ Jesus

All of these phrases have something to do with how God makes us spiritually alive.

Purpose Phrases

2. Look at the verse below and underline one or two words that draw your attention.

For we are God's workmanship, created in Christ Jesus to do good works, which God prepared in advance for us to do. (verse 10)

3. Do the words you underlined fit with what you think God has been doing in your life? If so, how?

Grace

4. The word *grace* appears three times in this passage (verses 5,7,8), and the phrase "by grace you have been saved" appears twice (verses 5,8). God's grace is interwoven throughout our lives, if we have the eyes to see it. How do you sense the presence of God's grace in your life?

☐ when I make mistakes
☐ in my desires to serve
☐ not holding grudges against people
☐ responsible for the good that comes about in my life
☐ other:

Christ

5. The word that appears most frequently in this passage is *Christ* (verses 5, 6, 7). Being made alive—having a spiritual awakening—is about Christ. Ponder for a moment the simplicity of that.

Picturing the Passage   10-15 minutes

If you were to draw a picture of this passage (do that, if you wish), you might draw Christ handing out gifts. Those gifts might include spiritual awakening, God's great love, God's rich mercy, His kindness, faith, being raised up with Christ, being seated with Him in the heavenly realms, and being His workmanship.

For example, if you have struggled with a certain sin, you might find yourself picturing a gift of "incomparable riches of his grace." Or if you have watched a friend die and now fear your own death, you might ponder a gift of being "seated with him in the heavenly realms in Christ Jesus."

Read the passage aloud this time and then close your eyes, picturing Christ giving you one or two of these gifts. If you wish, hold out your hands, palms upward, as a symbolic gesture of receiving that gift.

❶ Have group members read the above information. Then ask one person to read the passage aloud as other group members picture Christ giving them gifts.

Soaking In the Passage   5-15 minutes

Read the passage aloud again and ponder the following question for a few minutes: *What word or image from the passage touches my life today?* Write that word or image in the space below.

Word or image:

❶ Have a different group member read the passage aloud and then state the question printed in italics. Ask them to write their responses when they're ready. After several minutes of silence, ask each group member to read what they've written.

Pondering the Invitation   5-15 minutes

Perhaps God is offering you an invitation in this passage: *What do I sense this passage calling me to do, or what do I sense this passage asking me to receive from God?* Sit quietly for a few minutes, pondering those questions. If something comes to you right away, set that aside and see what else occurs to you. If nothing comes at all, rest in that. It may come to mind later today or during the week ahead.

❶ Read the above instructions aloud and after a few minutes, repeat the question printed in italics. Ask group members to respond by saying, "I sense this passage calling me to. . . ." Then complete that statement with a short phrase. Anyone who wishes to pass may do so.

Praying   5-10 minutes

Respond to God by telling Him how you feel about what you sensed or didn't sense during this meditation. If you need to present questions to God, do so.

❶ After allowing a few minutes for private prayer, ask group members to pray silently for the group as a whole regarding their desire to love God.

Daily Lectio

If you wish, use the above format to meditate on God's Word between group meetings. You may wish to focus on today's passage every day this week, or you can use the following passages:

- John 1:14-17 (the Word dwelling with us in the fullness of His grace)
- 1 Corinthians 15:50-58 (how we'll be clothed with immortality)
- 2 Corinthians 9:7-15 (how God gives us gifts and helps us serve)
- 2 Corinthians 12:9-10 (how God's grace helps us)
- Ephesians 1:17-23 (God's gift of the riches of His glorious inheritance in the saints)
- Hebrews 4:14-16 (approaching God's throne of grace)

God Changes My Character
Genesis 32:9-12,24-30

❶ After group members have had a chance to greet each other, read the centering instructions in the "Warming Up" section. Then present the question and let them reflect quietly for a few minutes. Repeat the question and ask them to share their thoughts in a sentence or two. Anyone who wishes to pass may do so.

Warming Up   5-10 minutes
Center yourself by slowly breathing in and out several times. Relax your neck and then take time to let your other muscles relax. Offer your distracting thoughts to God, one by one.

Consider this quiet question: When have I wrestled with God within myself— or could have but didn't? Close your eyes and take a few minutes to consider your past experiences and the pressing needs in your life. If an answer doesn't come to you at this time, that's fine. Try to enjoy God's presence without having to do anything.

Reading the Passage   15-20 minutes
As you read the Scripture passage aloud, set aside what you've heard before about this passage and try to look at it in a fresh way. Note the explanations in the shaded box.

Genesis 32:9-12,24-30

JACOB PRAYS
⁹Then Jacob prayed, "O God of my father Abraham, God of my father Isaac, O LORD, who said to me, 'Go back to your country and your

relatives, and I will make you prosper,' [10]I am unworthy of all the kindness and faithfulness you have shown your servant. I had only my staff when I crossed this Jordan, but now I have become two groups. [11]*Save me,* I pray, *from the hand of my brother Esau, for I am afraid* he will come and attack me, and also the mothers with their children. [12]But you have said, 'I will surely make you prosper and will make your descendants like the sand of the sea, which cannot be counted.' "

JACOB WRESTLES

[24]So Jacob was left alone, and *a man* wrestled with him till daybreak. [25] When the man saw that he could not overpower him, he touched the socket of Jacob's hip so that his hip was wrenched as he wrestled with the man. [26]Then the man said, "Let me go, for it is daybreak."

But Jacob replied, "I will not let you go unless you bless me."

[27]The man asked him, "What is your name?"

"Jacob," he answered.

[28]Then the man said, *"Your name will no longer be Jacob, but Israel,* because you have struggled with God and with men and have overcome."

[29]Jacob said, "Please tell me your name."

But he replied, "Why do you ask my name?" Then he blessed him there.

[30]So Jacob called the place Peniel, saying, "It is because I saw God face to face, and yet my life was spared."

Read the notes in the shaded box, then take a moment to consider the following questions.

❶ After the passage is read, ask group members to read the explanations in the shaded box and then jot down answers to the questions below. After a few minutes, have them choose one question and share their answer in a sentence or two. Anyone who wishes to pass may do so. Explain that this is not a time for discussion but for reporting responses to the questions.

Save me from the hand of my brother Esau, for I am afraid—Twenty years before, Jacob gained Esau's birthright by fraud and cheated him out of his father's intended blessing (25:33, 27:27-40). Esau plotted revenge and Jacob fled. He was now seeing Esau again for the first time.

A man—This man appears to have been a supernatural being. He wrestled for hours without tiring; he dislocated Jacob's hip with a touch; instead of telling Jacob his name, he asked a question to indicate that Jacob should already know his identity. Later, Jacob considered that he had seen the face of God (verse 30). Hosea 12:3 refers to the man as an angel.

Your name will no longer be Jacob, but Israel—A name change in the ancient Middle East marked a significant change in the person's life. The name Jacob meant "deceiver," but Israel meant "he struggles with God."

Exploring the Angelic Encounter

1. When faced with the crisis of meeting his brother, whom he tricked, Jacob chose to ask the angel for a blessing (verse 26). Consider a current situation that is your fault. If an angel appeared to you in the midst of it, what would you ask of that angel?

2. The way in which God dealt with Jacob is not easy to understand. Why wrestle with an angel? God simply spoke conversationally to Abraham and Elijah, but with Jacob he used dreams and wrestling matches to engage him. But Jacob was a competitive man, good at outdoing others—"wrestling," so to speak, with people in difficult situations. Suppose an angel appeared to you (although you wouldn't be sure if this person was an angel). How would this angel be wise to engage you to get your attention?

   ☐ meet you on a walk, keep walking with you
   ☐ challenge you to a table game
   ☐ start a conversation with you
   ☐ ask you to dance
   ☐ talk with you as a temporary "consultant" at work
   ☐ make a surprising comment to you, acting as a clerk in a grocery store
   ☐ other:

3. If God were going to give you some new names, based on your current progress with Him, what would those names be?

	NAME BASED ON FORMER CHARACTER I used to be a . . .	NAME BASED ON CURRENT PROGRESS WITH GOD I now am one who . . .
JACOB: ISRAEL	"deceiver" (Jacob)	"struggles with God" (Israel)
EXAMPLE:	"whiner"	"cries out to God"
YOU:		
YOU:		
YOU:		

Picturing the Passage   10-15 minutes
Before reading the passage again, consider these cues.

Character Cue: Jacob and His Slow Progress
Little faith—All of his life, Jacob had been good at getting what he wanted from his mother, his father, his brother, and even from a difficult person such as his father-in-law, Laban (Genesis 25-31).

More faith—While escaping from Esau twenty years earlier, Jacob had experienced a divinely inspired dream of a stairway with angels coming up and down, and he been given promises by God. His response—a vow—indicates that he mustered as much faith as he could: "If God will be with me and will watch over me . . . [he named many conditions God had to meet] . . . then the LORD will be my God." He showed cautious faith—"If . . ."—and gave God conditions to meet (Genesis 28:1-22).

Mature faith—In today's passage, Jacob prayed a contrite prayer full of praise, confession, thankfulness, requests, and references to God's promises. He seemed to realize that nothing would work out without God's input.

Setting Cue: Riverbank Location

Jacob was alone in the grasslands by the bank of the Jabbok River. Foxes, wolves, and jackals, as well as snakes and scorpions, were common, and Jacob, a tent dweller, was outside alone.

Picture Jacob. How do you think he stood? Walked? He was obviously assertive and knew how to make things go his way—a wrestling match kind of guy. Once you've got him fixed in the picturing part of your brain, read the text again. As you do, picture Jacob:

- praying in fear and distress (verses 9-12)
- wrestling all night with an angel (verses 24-25)
- pressing the angel for a blessing (verses 26-29)

Read the passage aloud this time and then close your eyes, picturing Jacob alone in the grasslands. Smell the grass and the river. Hear the sounds of the animals at night. Wonder with him, *Who is this strange man approaching?* How does the wrestling match begin?

❶ Have group members read the cues silently. Then have a group member read the passage aloud while the others picture the passage.

Soaking In the Passage   5-15 minutes

Reflect on how your life is touched today by this passage about Jacob. Read the passage aloud again and ponder the following questions for a few minutes: *If I were to spend the night alone by a river, what would I need to say to God? What word, phrase, scene, or feeling from the passage stays with me?*

After a few minutes, write about the word, phrase, scene, or feeling that resonates within you from the passage.

Word or phrase:

Scene or feeling: *Within Jacob's experience, I see . . .*

> ❶ Have a different group member read the passage aloud and then state the question printed in italics. Have the group sit together quietly, and then write about the word, phrase, scene, or image that comes to mind. After a few minutes, ask group members to read what they've written. Anyone who wishes to pass may do so.

Pondering the Invitation   5-15 minutes

Perhaps God is offering you an invitation in this passage to do or be something within the next few days. What might that be? Sit in silence for a few minutes, pondering this question: *What do I sense this passage calling me to do or be or know?* If nothing comes to you, thank God for working with all kinds of people.

> ❶ Read the above instructions aloud, and after a few minutes, repeat the question printed in italics. Ask group members to respond by saying, "I sense this passage calling me to. . . ." Then complete that statement with a short phrase. Anyone who wishes to pass may do so.

Praying   5-10 minutes

Take a few minutes to respond to God. How do you feel about what you sensed (or didn't sense)? What do you most want to say to God at this time?

> ❶ After allowing a few minutes for private prayer, ask group members to pray for the person on their left. Anyone wishing to pray silently may do so by saying, "I'm praying silently," then signifying when he or she is finished by saying "Amen."

Daily Lectio

If you wish, use the above format to meditate on God's Word between group meetings. You may wish to focus on today's passage every day this week, or you can use the following passages:

- Genesis 28:10-16 (Jacob's dream of the stairway)
- Genesis 32:6-12, 24-31 (same story, but ponder the significance of Jacob's limp, verse 31)
- Psalm 13:1-6 (wrestling with God's silence)
- Psalm 38:15-22 (calling on God for strength and help)
- Ephesians 6:12-18 (struggling with the Enemy)
- 1 Timothy 6:11-16 (character qualities we are to pursue)

PART THREE

HEALING LIFE'S WOUNDS

When You Sense God Speaking to Your Deeper Hurts

What If Nothing Happens in the Silence?

The times of quiet in these sessions may feel like a waste of time at first. You may think nothing important is happening, but you are connecting with God and training yourself to expect God to speak to you. A. W. Tozer advised, "[The Bible] is not only a book which was once spoken, but a book which is now speaking. . . . If you would follow on to know the Lord, come at once to the open Bible, expecting it to speak to you."[1]

Don't be concerned if nothing seems to happen. The act of meditation is not something you can control. Let God do it. Thelma Hall wrote that "we will never be 'in charge' in prayer if it is real."[2] At first the result of your meditation may be "underwhelming." You may think, *That was all? No new deep facts? No new insights?* If your mind wanders during the time of quiet, peek at the subheadings within the text or reread the Cultural Cues in Picturing the Passage, and then close your eyes again.

The quiet after reading the passage gives the truth of the passage a chance to resonate in your subconscious, which constantly collects data for further use. Storing it there is a good idea because, in the midst of temptations and doubts, these truths come back in unselfconscious nudges.

Let the days pass. Quiet rumination on the Word makes truth and love digestible to a heart of stone that previously could not fathom how certain truths could be believed or an enemy could be loved.

---

1. A. W. Tozer, *The Pursuit of God* (Camp Hill, Penn.: Christian Publications, 1982), pp. 81-82.
2. Thelma Hall, *Too Deep for Words: Rediscovering Lectio Divina* (New York: Paulist Press, 1988), p. 32.

God Sees My Hurt
Mark 5:22-34

❶ After group members have had a chance to greet each other, read the centering instructions in the "Warming Up" section (see bullets). Then read the quoted material and sit quietly together for a few minutes before going on to "Reading the Passage."

Warming Up   5-10 minutes
The following comments were written about today's passage, which describes when Jesus talked with a woman in the middle of a crowd. Let these words prepare you for your conversation with God about this passage of Scripture.

> From the moment Jesus was face to face with the woman, there seems to be nobody there but He and she. It happened in the middle of the crowd; but the crowd was forgotten and Jesus spoke to that woman and treated her as if she was the only person in the world.[1]

Close your eyes and picture yourself standing or sitting face-to-face with Jesus. There's nobody else there. Reflect on this silently for about five minutes, using the following techniques to center yourself:

- Breathe in and out deeply five or six times. Relax your neck and move it around. Then let your arms go limp and relax your legs and ankles. Relax each part from the inside out.
- Use the "palms down, palms up" method (described in the introduction) to turn your distractions over to God. Rest your hands in your lap, placing the palms down whenever you think of concerns you need to turn over to God. Turn your palms up as a symbol of your desire to receive from the Lord and set aside distractions.

Reading the Passage   15-20 minutes
Read the Scripture passage silently, noting the explanations in the shaded box.

❶ Ask a group member to read the Scripture passage aloud. Suggest that other group members close their eyes while they listen.

Mark 5:22-34

"STEALING" A CURE

²²Then one of the synagogue rulers, named Jairus, came there. Seeing Jesus, he fell at his feet ²³and pleaded earnestly with him, "My little daughter is dying. Please come and put your hands on her so that she will be healed and live." ²⁴So Jesus went with him.

A large crowd followed and pressed around him. ²⁵And a woman was there who had been *subject to bleeding for twelve years.* ²⁶She had suffered a great deal under the care of many doctors and had spent all she had, yet instead of getting better she grew worse. ²⁷When she heard about Jesus, she came up behind him in the crowd and touched his cloak, ²⁸because she thought, "If I just touch his clothes, I will be healed." ²⁹Immediately her bleeding stopped and she felt in her body that she was freed from her suffering.

REVEALING HER PROBLEM

³⁰At once Jesus realized that power had gone out from him. He turned around in the crowd and asked, *"Who touched my clothes?"*

³¹"You see the people crowding against you," his disciples answered, "and yet you can ask, 'Who touched me?'"

³²But Jesus kept looking around to see who had done it. ³³Then the woman, knowing what had happened to her, came and fell at his feet and, trembling with fear, told him the whole truth. ³⁴He said to her, "Daughter, your faith has healed you. Go in peace and be freed from your suffering."

If you haven't read the notes in the shaded box, read them silently now. Take a minute to consider the following questions.

Subject to bleeding for twelve years —This would have made her ritually unclean (Leviticus 15:25-27) and excluded her from social contact.

Who touched my clothes? —Some people believe He may not have known who did it, or He may have known but wanted them to meet face-to-face, or He knew it was important

❶ After the passage is read aloud, ask group members to read the explanations in the shaded box and jot down answers to the questions below. After a few minutes, have them choose one question and share their answer in a sentence or two. Anyone who wishes to pass may do so. Remind the group that this is not a time for discussion but for reporting responses to the questions.

The Woman's Desperation

1. This woman had many reasons to be desperate:

- She had visited many doctors (the Talmud gives eleven cures for continuous hemorrhaging—tonics; astringents; even superstitions, such as carrying an ostrich egg in a linen rag in summer and in a cotton rag in winter).[2]
- She had spent all the money she had.
- She had gotten worse instead of better.

She must have debated within herself whether she should approach Jesus. Jot down a few possible arguments for and against approaching Him.

For Approaching Jesus	*Against* Approaching Jesus
1.	1.
2.	2.

2. Imagine for a moment that this woman had the same personality and temperament as you. For which of the following reasons would she have touched Jesus' clothes to find a cure?

- ☐ superstition (thinking His clothes were wired with power)
- ☐ timidity (unwilling to speak up and ask for help)
- ☐ embarrassment (unwilling to speak about such an ailment in public)
- ☐ concern for Jesus (not wanting Him to become unclean by touching her to heal her)
- ☐ desperation (she did what it took to get around the problem of all the people who were vying for Jesus' attention)

Telling the Whole Truth

3. What topics besides the following could the "whole truth" have included?

Then the woman, knowing what had happened to her, came and fell at His feet and, trembling with fear, told him the whole truth. (verse 33)

- that she was the one who had touched His clothes
- why she had touched His clothes instead of talking to Him
- her medical history: how many doctors she'd seen, how much money she'd spent
- the effects of having been unclean for twelve years: not being touched for years; looked down upon as unclean; unable to join in worship
- other reasons:

4. What do you think it was about the presence of Christ that caused a woman to give details (the "whole truth") publicly about a personal problem, when a few minutes before she couldn't even present herself to Jesus?

5. In what way was the fact that she told the "whole truth" part of her healing?

If any of the above questions are too difficult to answer right now, hold them before God for a few minutes and then go on. Don't worry about getting an answer, but be open to what may come to you in the next few days.

Picturing the Passage   10-15 minutes
Before you read the passage again, consider the Cultural Cue. Let it help set the scene of how this event in Scripture might have occurred.

> ❶ Have group members read the Cultural Cue silently and ponder the suggested questions. Then ask a group member to read the passage aloud while the others picture the passage.

Cultural Cue: The "Cloak"
Men wore an inner garment close to the skin and an outer garment wrapped at the waist with a *girdle*—a wide cloth or leather belt. According to Jewish law (Numbers 15:37-40, Deuteronomy 22:12), this outer garment was supposed to have two fringes hung at the bottom and two hung over the shoulders where the cloak folded over. The woman probably touched the fringes on Jesus' cloak. In addition, great teachers whom the Jews considered rabbis (Jesus was called "rabbi," John 1:49, 6:25) also wore a *tallith*—a rectangular or square outer garment worn over the top of the body. This had a tassel or fringe at each of its four corners.[3]

Now that you've considered this cue, take a few minutes to quiet yourself again and read the passage aloud this time. Close your eyes and picture the events as if they were a movie playing in your mind. If you wish, consider the next two questions as you sit in the quiet.

1. Put yourself in the place of the woman—you're in the middle of a noisy, teeming crowd. Your nostrils are full of the perspiration of others and of your own disease. What is the best thing about Jesus?

2. Later, when everyone in the crowd is looking at you, what is the best thing about Jesus now?

Soaking In the Passage

5-15 minutes

Consider this all-important question you should ask whenever you read Scripture: *How is my life touched by this passage today?* Read the passage aloud again and ponder the following question for a few minutes: *What phrase, scene, or dramatic moment emerges from the passage and stays with me?* If you latch on to something right away, set that aside for a minute and see if anything else emerges.

Here are some examples of phrases, scenes, or dramatic moments to consider:

■ the anxiety Jairus probably felt when Jesus delayed going with him to ask who had touched His clothing (verses 22-23,30-32)
■ after touching His clothing, the woman "felt in her body that she was freed from her suffering" (verse 29)
■ the woman standing in the crowd telling the "whole truth" (verse 33)
■ phrases (circle one): whole truth, go in peace, be freed from your suffering

After a few minutes, write about the phrase, scene, or moment in the passage that resonates within you.

Phrase:

Scene or moment:

I hear . . . I see . . .

❶ Ask a group member to read the passage aloud and then state the question printed in italics. Ask the group to fill in the word or phrase that sticks with them. After a few minutes, ask group members to read what they've written. Anyone who wishes to pass may do so.

Pondering the Invitation   5-15 minutes

Perhaps God is offering you an invitation in this passage to do or be something within the next few days. What might that be? Sit quietly for a few minutes, pondering this question: *What do I sense God saying to me in this passage?*

❶ Read the above instructions aloud and repeat the question printed in italics. Ask group members to respond by saying, "I sense this passage calling me to. . . ." Then complete that statement with a short phrase. Anyone who wishes to pass may do so.

Praying   5-10 minutes

Take a few minutes to respond to God about this Scripture passage. How do you feel about what you sensed (or didn't sense)? What is it you most want to say to God at this time?

❶ After allowing a few minutes for private prayer, ask group members to pray for the person on their left. Anyone wishing to pray silently may do so by saying, "I'm praying silently." They can signify when they are finished by saying "Amen."

Daily Lectio

If you wish, use the above format to meditate on God's Word between group meetings. You may want to focus on today's passage every day this week (try using a different version of the Bible besides NIV), or you can use the following passages:

- Psalm 6:1-7 (asking God for healing)
- Psalm 30:1-10 (praising God for healing, rescuing, and showing favor)
- Psalm 41:1-4 (how God restores us)
- Matthew 9:18-26 (a parallel passage—seeing the same events through different eyes)
- Luke 8:41-56 (a parallel passage—the same events through different eyes)
- James 5:16 (how confession of sin helps healing)

1. William Barclay, *The Daily Bible Study: The Gospel of Luke* (PA: Westminster Press, 1956), p. 114.
2. Barclay, p. 128.
3. Alfred Edersheim, *The Life and Times of Jesus the Messiah* (MA: Hendrickson Publishers, 1993), pp. 428-429.

Developing a Satisfied Heart

Luke 12:22-34

---

❶ After your group has had a chance to greet each other, read the centering instructions in the "Warming Up" section. After they have sat in silence for a few minutes, ask them to describe for the group, in five words or less, the worry they turned over to God.

Warming Up   5-10 minutes

Center yourself by breathing in and out several times. Relax your neck and then take time to relax other muscles.

As you quiet yourself, use the "palms up, palms down" method. (Rest your hands in your lap, placing the palms down whenever you think of concerns you need to turn over to God. Turn your palms up as a symbol of your desire to receive from the Lord.) Only this time, look for worries that need to be turned upward. If you run out of worries, simply sit for a few minutes with your palms turned up.

If your mind wanders, use a key word, such as *God* or *peace* or *surrender* to pull your thoughts back to the symbolic turning over of your worries to God.

Reading the Passage   15-20 minutes

If you've read this passage before, try to read it silently now with fresh eyes. Note the explanation in the shaded box.

---

❶ Ask a group member to read the Scripture passage aloud. Suggest that other group members close their eyes as they listen.

Luke 12:22-34

²²Then Jesus said to his disciples: "Therefore I tell you, do not worry about your life, what you will eat; or about your body, what you will

91

wear. [23]Life is more than food, and the body more than clothes. [24]Consider the ravens: They do not sow or reap, they have no storeroom or barn; yet God feeds them. And how much more valuable you are than birds! [25]Who of you by worrying can add a single hour to his life? [26]Since you cannot do this very little thing, why do you worry about the rest?

[27]"Consider how the lilies grow. They do not labor or spin. Yet I tell you, not even *Solomon in all his splendor* was dressed like one of these. [28]If that is how God clothes the grass of the field, which is here today, and tomorrow is thrown into the fire, how much more will he clothe you, O you of little faith!

THE FOCUSED HEART

[29]And do not set your heart on what you will eat or drink; do not worry about it. [30]For the pagan world runs after all such things, and your Father knows that you need them. [31]But seek his kingdom, and these things will be given to you as well.

[32]Do not be afraid, little flock, for your Father has been pleased to give you the kingdom. [33]Sell your possessions and give to the poor. Provide purses for yourselves that will not wear out, a treasure in heaven that will not be exhausted, where no thief comes near and no moth destroys. [34]For where your treasure is, there your heart will be also.

If you haven't read the note in the shaded box, read it silently now. Take a minute to consider the following questions.

❶ After reading the passage, ask group members to read the explanation in the shaded box and jot down answers to the questions below. After a few minutes, ask them to choose one question and share their answer in a sentence or two. Anyone who wishes to pass may do so. Explain that this is not a time for discussion but for reporting responses to the questions.

Contrasts and Images

1. Consider these two humorous images extracted from this passage:

■ somebody tallying up the additional hours they can live because they invested their time worrying
■ people adoring lilies more than the most popular movie star

Use some blank space in this book to draw one of these images as a cartoon.

Solomon in all his splendor—Solomon was considered a fashionable, glamorous person. To get the meaning, we might substitute the name of a well-known celebrity or fashion model.

2. Consider the following paradoxes extracted from this passage:

■ ravens that store up nothing, yet have what they need
■ treasure that is safe from theft or destruction
■ purses that don't wear out

These are paradoxes because they make us ask, *How can this be?* How can a raven store nothing yet have necessities? How can treasure be burglar-proof? How can a purse, worn often for buying and trading, not get old and develop holes through which your money slips? These paradoxes cannot be explained because they are provisions of God. They are mysteries, just as God's provision for us today is also full of mystery.

Consider something you worry about (getting all your errands run, staying physically fit, having sufficient retirement funds, resolving problems with other people, raising kids who succeed in life) and make up a mysterious solution to it.

WORRY	PARADOXICAL IMAGE
How will I get all these errands run in an hour?	looking out your door and seeing lined up: the dry cleaner with your clothes, the bank teller with your money, the grocery clerk with a quart of milk, the veterinarian giving shots to your cat
How will I stay physically fit?	an adult body that keeps replenishing and growing, even when you're asleep (a child's body does this)
Will I have sufficient retirement funds?	a pension that doubles every time you take a sick day
Your worry:	
Your worry:	

The paradoxical solutions you thought of give you an idea of how Jesus' listeners felt when they heard His ideas. They also give you a keener admiration for the mysteries of heaven.

3. Part of our problem when we worry is that we aren't seeking God's kingdom or treasuring what God treasures. Jesus said to His listeners, "Life is more than

food, and the body more than clothes" (verse 23). If Jesus had spoken that verse to you, He would have known what you treasure and probably included it.

Complete that verse the way Jesus might have said it to you:

Life is more than _____. Use the check boxes, if you like, and mark as many as are appropriate.

☐ food
☐ clothing
☐ having a cushioned retirement
☐ being a perfect parent, spouse, coworker
☐ having a body others admire
☐ scratching off every item on today's "to do" list
☐ other:
☐ other:

Heart Conditions

4. Jesus seems preoccupied with the heart. He tells His listeners where to "set their hearts" and asks them to look at where their heart "is." The Greek word for heart, *kardia,* came to stand for a person's "mental and moral activity, both the rational and emotional elements. . . . The heart is used figuratively for the hidden springs of the personal life."[1]

   Read the verses below and try to list at least six words that you could substitute for the word *heart* in these verses. (For example, the word *energy* could be substituted for *heart* in these verses.)

   [29]And do not set your heart on what you will eat or drink; do not worry about it.
   [34]For where your treasure is, there your heart will be also.

   ■ List of word substitutes:

5. The left-hand column below lists what the satisfied heart believes, based on what today's passage says. Fill in the blanks in the right-hand column with the ideas that cause us to worry.

THE SATISFIED HEART BELIEVES	THE WORRYING HEART BELIEVES
God will provide whatever is needed.	
Life is more than food anyway.	
If I seek His kingdom, all the food and drink I need will be provided.	
God provides treasures that can't be taken away.	

Picturing the Passage   10-15 minutes

Review the chart above one more time. Then read the Bible passage aloud and consider the question: *What does the satisfied heart look like?* (Use any words you like. For example, you can use a color or feeling or action.)

❶ Read the instructions above and ask a group member to read the passage aloud for the group.

Soaking In the Passage   5-15 minutes

Reflect on how this passage touches your life today. Read the passage aloud again and ponder the following question for several minutes: *What word or contrast or image from this passage stays with me?* If something comes to mind immediately, set it aside for a moment and see if anything else emerges.

After a few minutes, write the word or image that resonates within you from the passage. Or, if you wish, go back to the humorous image you drew in Question 1 (Reading the Passage), and change it or add to it.

Word, contrast, image:

❶ Ask a group member to read the passage aloud and then state the question printed in italics. Have the group sit quietly together for a while and then fill in the blank or add to their drawing from question 1. After a few minutes, ask each group member to read what they've written. Anyone who wishes to pass may do so.

Pondering the Invitation   5-15 minutes

Perhaps God is offering you an invitation in this passage to do or be something within the next few days. What might that be? Sit in the silence for a few minutes and ponder this question: *What do I need to know from God about having a satisfied heart?*

❶ Read the above instructions aloud and repeat the question printed in italics. Ask group members to respond by saying, "I sense this passage calling me to know. . . ." Then complete that statement with a short phrase. Anyone who wishes to pass may do so.

Praying   5-10 minutes

Take a few minutes to respond to God about the satisfied heart. How do you feel about what you sensed? What do you most want to say to God at this time?

❶ After allowing a few minutes for private prayer, ask group members to pray for the person on their left. Anyone wishing to pray silently may do so by saying, "I'm praying silently," and signifying when he or she is finished by saying "Amen."

Daily Lectio

If you wish, use the above format to meditate on God's Word between group meetings. You may wish to focus on today's passage every day this week, or you can use the following passages:

■ Psalm 16:7-11 (feeling secure in God)
■ Psalm 19:8-14 (trust in God is more precious than gold)
■ Psalm 27:7-14 (how God helps me face fears)
■ Proverbs 2:1-10 (the wise ear and understanding heart)
■ Proverbs 14:29-33 (the peaceful heart)
■ John 14:25-27 (how Christ gives peace)

---

1. W. E. Vine, Merrill F. and Unger, William White, *Vine's Expository Dictionary of Biblical Words* (Nashville: Thomas Nelson, 1985), p. 297.

Willing to Be Healed

John 5:1-9

Jesus challenges the man who had been disabled for thirty-eight years

❶ After group members have had a chance to greet each other, read the centering instructions in the "Warming Up" section. Then present the quiet question. You may want to set the tone by praying aloud: "Help us, O God, to set aside what is around us and invite You to the center of our being." Let group members reflect quietly for a few minutes and then repeat the question. Ask them to share their thoughts in a sentence or two. Anyone who wishes to pass may do so.

Warming Up   5-10 minutes

Center yourself by breathing in and out several times. Relax your neck and then take time to relax your other muscles. Turn over each distraction, jotting it down, if necessary, to surrender it. Ask yourself the following question to help focus your thoughts for meditation on today's passage: In what areas of life am I at a standstill? Why?

Close your eyes and take a few minutes to quietly consider this question. It's okay if nothing comes to mind right away. Just enjoy being in God's presence.

Reading the Passage   15-20 minutes

Read the Scripture passage silently, noting the explanations in the shaded box.

❶ Ask a group member to read the Scripture passage aloud. Suggest that other group members close their eyes as they listen.

John 5:1-9

JESUS GOES TO THE PLACE OF NEED

[1]Some time later, Jesus went up to Jerusalem for a feast of the Jews. [2]Now there is in Jerusalem near the Sheep Gate a pool, which in Aramaic is called Bethesda and which is surrounded by five covered colonnades. [3]Here a *great number of disabled people* used to lie—the blind, the lame, the paralyzed. [5]One who was there had been an invalid for thirty-eight years.

JESUS SPEAKS WITH THE DISABLED MAN

[6]When Jesus saw him lying there and learned that he had been in this condition for a long time, he asked him, "Do you want to get well?"

[7]"Sir," the invalid replied, "I have no one to help me into the pool when the water is stirred. While I am trying to get in, someone else goes down ahead of me."

JESUS INVITES HIM TO WALK

[8]Then Jesus said to him, "Get up! Pick up your mat and walk." [9]At once the man was *cured;* he picked up his mat and walked.

If you haven't read the notes in the shaded box at the bottom of this page, read them now. Take a minute to consider the following questions.

> ❶ After reading the passage, ask group members to read the explanations in the shaded box and jot down answers to the following questions. After a few minutes, have them choose one question and share their answer in a sentence or two. Anyone who wishes to pass may do so. Explain that this is not a time for discussion but for reporting responses to the questions.

Willingness

1. This man didn't approach Jesus and didn't ask to be healed. In fact, Jesus challenged the man who had been disabled for thirty-eight years by asking, "Do you want to get well?" Jesus' question has made people speculate that the man

---

Great number of disabled people—Jesus may have healed many or all of these people, but John chose to tell about this one healing because of the heat it generated later among the Pharisees (John 5:10-15).

Cured—This cure was complex: his physical disability was cured, as well as thirty-eight years of deterioration of muscle and bone. After not being upright on one's feet for a few weeks, people often can't stand without fainting. This man stood and walked, apparently without limping, fainting, or falling.

no longer wanted to help himself. He may have felt trapped and helpless and was no longer willing to try. It's difficult to tell. The man didn't answer Jesus' question directly but gave an explanation of why he hadn't been healed through the pool.

When, if ever, have you gotten so used to a bad situation that you quit trying to resolve it?

2. Consider the disabled man's reply, "I have no one to help me." Perhaps you've had a similar experience — no friend or relative to count on, or you lack the resources to solve your problem. List a few areas in your life that are at a standstill. You would resolve these situations, if you had the following:

■

■

3. Pick one of your two answers from question 2 and consider Jesus' question: "Do you want help?" Are you sure you should pursue this?

☐ Yes, I'm anxious to resolve this.
☐ If I thought it would work, I would try.
☐ I'm not sure.
☐ Other:

(If you wish, write about this in the blank space at the end of this session.)

4. If you want to resolve the situation, are you willing to take a risk?

☐ The right thing would be to be willing, but I'm not sure I am.
☐ No, I've already tried so hard. I can't risk another failure.
☐ Other:

(If you wish, write about this in the blank space at the end of this session.)

Picturing the Passage   10-15 minutes
Before reading the passage again, consider the setting cue.

❶ Have group members read the setting cue silently. Then ask a group member to read the Scripture passage aloud while the others picture the events and conversation.

Setting Cue: The Pool of Bethesda

This event took place at a sheep gate in Jerusalem's huge city wall by a pool with five porches. Historians can't identify this structure for certain, so we don't know what it looked like. It may have been a gazebo-type structure with a pentagon-shaped border and a pool in the middle. Today in Jerusalem, there are mineral springs on the east side of the city, and the pool may have been fed by one of them.[1] This might explain the stirring of the water and its reputation for curing. The bed the disabled man picked up was probably a mat of woven fabric or cloth.

Read the passage aloud and close your eyes, picturing the events as if they were a movie playing in your mind. Consider putting yourself in the place of the man who was healed. If you wish, contrast how you feel when Christ prods you about being willing to "walk" and how it feels to actually get up and "walk."

Soaking In the Passage   5-15 minutes

Ponder how this passage touches your life today. Read the passage aloud again and reflect on the following question for several minutes: *What phrase or scene emerges from the passage and stays with me?* Here are some possibilities:

☐ phrases (circle one): Thirty-eight years; no one to help me.
☐ question: Do you want to get well?
☐ scene: He picked up his mat and walked.

After a few minutes, write a phrase or describe a scene from the passage that stays with you.
Phrase or scene:

❶ Ask a group member to read the Scripture passage aloud and state the question printed in italics. Have the group sit quietly and then fill in the blanks above. After a few minutes, ask group members to read what they've written. Anyone who wishes to pass may do so.

Pondering the Invitation   5-15 minutes

Perhaps God is offering you an invitation in this passage to do or be something within the next few days. What might that be? Sit quietly for a few minutes, pondering this question: *What do I need to know, do, or be in order to "get well"?*

❶ Read the above instructions aloud and repeat the question printed in italics. Ask group members to respond by saying, "I sense this passage calling me to. . . ." Then complete that statement with a short phrase. Anyone who wishes to pass may do so.

Praying

Take a few minutes to respond to God about this meditation. How do you feel about what you sensed (or didn't sense)? What is it you most want to say to God at this time?

❶ After allowing a few minutes for private prayer, ask group members to pray for the person on their left. Anyone wishing to pray silently may do so by saying, "I'm praying silently," then signifying when he or she is finished by saying "Amen."

Daily Lectio

If you wish, use the above format to meditate on God's Word between group meetings. You may wish to focus on today's passage every day this week, or you can use the following passages:

- Mark 7:31-37 (Jesus heals a deaf-mute)
- Luke 5:17-25 (Jesus heals a paralytic)
- Luke 6:6-11 (Jesus heals a man's shriveled hand)
- Luke 7:1-10 (Jesus heals a centurion's servant)
- Luke 13:10-17 (Jesus heals a crippled woman)
- John 9:1-9 (Jesus heals a man born blind)

---

1. Frederic Louis Godet, *Commentary on John's Gospel* (Grand Rapids: Kregal Publications, 1978), p.455.

God Turns Mourning into Dancing

Psalm 30:1-12

❶ After group members have had a chance to greet each other, read the "Warming Up" instructions. Then present the quiet question and let them think about it for a few minutes. Repeat the question and ask them to share their thoughts in a sentence or two. Anyone who wishes to pass may do so.

Warming Up   5-10 minutes

To prepare for this meditation, center yourself by breathing in and out several times. Relax your neck and then take time to relax the other muscles in your body. Turn each distracting thought over to God. Ask yourself the following quiet question to help focus your thoughts for meditation on today's passage: In what ways does God lift us up? Sit quietly for several minutes without worrying about coming up with a great insight. One simple word or phrase may come to mind, or perhaps you can just enjoy God's presence, knowing that God has lifted you up many times in the past.

Reading the Passage   15-20 minutes

Silently read the following passage, noting the explanations in the shaded box.

❶ Ask a group member to read aloud the following passage. Suggest that other group members close their eyes as they listen.

Psalm 30:1-12

A song. For the *dedication of the temple.* Of David.

HOW GOD RESCUED ME

¹I will exalt you, O LORD,
    for you lifted me out of the *depths*
    and did not let my enemies gloat over me.
²O LORD my God, I called to you for help
    and you healed me.
³O LORD, you brought me up from the grave;
    you spared me from going down into the pit.

ASKING OTHERS TO PRAISE GOD FOR THE RESCUE

⁴Sing to the LORD, you *saints* of his;
    praise his holy name.
⁵For his *anger lasts only a moment,*
    but his favor lasts a lifetime;
weeping may remain for a night,
    but rejoicing comes in the morning.

GOING OVER THE RESCUE AGAIN

⁶When I felt secure, I said,
    "I will never be shaken."
⁷O LORD, when you favored me,
    you *made my mountain stand firm;*
but when you hid your face,
    I was dismayed.

⁸To you, O LORD, I called;
    to the Lord I cried for mercy:
⁹"What gain is there in my destruction,
    in my going down into the pit?
Will the dust praise you?
    Will it proclaim your faithfulness?

Dedication of the temple — The site of the temple was the threshing floor of Araunah the Jebusite, where David built an altar to stop a plague on Israel (2 Samuel 24:18-25).

Depths — Seventy thousand Israelites died from the plague, which had come upon Israel because of David's actions. God rescued David and the rest of Israel from this death (2 Samuel 24:15).

Saints — Those who are committed to God.

Anger lasts only a moment — God's anger is not capricious, bad-tempered, or given to fits; it is a dimension of His justice and fairness. Like the sting of a shot or the temporary discomfort of an operation, God's anger (justice) does its work quickly.

Made my mountain stand firm — God made David feel secure.

Sackcloth — People in mourning tore their clothes and put coarse material around the waist next to the skin.

¹⁰Hear, O LORD, and be merciful to me;
  O LORD, be my help."

SUMMARY OF THE RESCUE

¹¹You turned my wailing into dancing;
  you removed my *sackcloth* and clothed me with joy,
¹²that my heart may sing to you and not be silent.
  O LORD my God, I will give you thanks forever.

If you haven't read the notes in the shaded box on the preceding page, read them now. Take a minute to consider the following questions.

❶ After reading the Scripture passage, ask group members to read the explanations in the shaded box and jot down answers to the questions below. After a few minutes, have them choose one question and share their answer in a sentence or two. Anyone who wishes to pass may do so. Explain that this is not a time for discussion but for reporting responses to the questions.

Mourning into Dancing

1. The outline headings for the Scripture passage show how David went over and over the events, describing the deliverance, asking others to celebrate it, and summarizing it again. We do the same thing when miraculous things happen. Look through the psalm again and underline the things God did. (For example, in verse 1, He "lifted me out of the depths." If you have trouble finding more examples, look at verses 1, 2, 3, 7, and 11.)

2. Circle what the psalmist did when he asked for help or felt he was in trouble. (For example, in verse 2, the psalmist said he called for help.)

3. Which of the following gifts would you like to receive from God's hand?

   ☐ being lifted out of the depths
   ☐ experiencing God's mercy
   ☐ assurance of His faithfulness
   ☐ feeling secure
   ☐ feeling spared
   ☐ having a heart that sings

4. Verses 1 and 2 indicate that when David was in his worst moment, he prayed. We've all prayed prayers of desperation, but how easy is it for us to pray honest prayers throughout our worst moments, especially when the worst moment is our fault? Check the appropriate box(es). I find prayer . . .

   ☐ difficult because praying is the last thing I think about doing
   ☐ difficult because I can't be that honest with God

☐ easier than it used to be
☐ almost a first impulse
☐ other:

Picturing the Passage   10-15 minutes

Before reading the passage again, consider the following cues.

> ❶ Have group members read the cues silently. Then have one group member read the
> Scripture passage aloud while the others picture the passage.

Character Cue: God and His Anger

David mentions God's anger (verse 5), and rightly so, for the plague was a part of David's punishment. What is God's anger like? "God's anger is not like man's anger. People often view God as a projection of their own personality. If you want to punch people when you get mad, you may assume God wants to do the same. If you sulk and turn anger inward, you may act as if God smolders at you.

"God's anger is different from man's anger: 'For I am God, and not man—the Holy One among you. I will not come in wrath' (Hosea 11:9). God gets angry in response to human moral lapses, but He doesn't have temper tantrums. Unlike us, He manages to be fair even when he's angry. God delights in showing mercy, not in showing off His power in irrational, thoughtless actions (Micah 7:18)."[1]

Setting Cue: The "Pit"

We don't know if David was on the brink of death or if he believed he deserved death because the plague was a result of his actions. Either way, it's likely that, with seventy thousand deaths, the pits he looked down into were mass graves. Even with relatives respectfully bringing their dead wrapped up, the scene must have been filled with weeping and the stench of death and disease. In this way, David looked into the face of death. It's riveting to think that he experienced God's mercy in such a full way during such terrible circumstances.

Now that you've looked at these cues, read the Scripture passage aloud, using the cues to picture David singing, dancing, and experiencing joy.

Soaking In the Passage   5-15 minutes

Consider how this passage touches your life today. Read it aloud again and ponder the following question: *What word or phrase, dramatic scene, sound, or smell emerges from the passage and stays with me?*

After a few minutes, write the word, phrase, images, or scenes that resonate within you from the passage.

Word or phrase:

Scene: I hear . . . I smell . . .

❶ Ask a group member to read the Scripture passage aloud and then read the question printed in italics. Have the group sit quietly and then fill in one of the blanks above. After a few minutes, ask group members to read what they've written. Anyone who wishes to pass may do so.

Pondering the Invitation   5-15 minutes
Perhaps God is offering you an invitation in this passage to do, be, feel, or realize something within the next few days. What might that be? Enjoy the silence for a few minutes, pondering this question: *What do I sense this passage calling me to do, be, feel, or realize?*

❶ Read the above instructions aloud and repeat the question printed in italics. Ask group members to respond by saying, "I sense this passage calling me to. . . ." Then complete that statement with a short phrase. Anyone who wishes to pass may do so.

Praying   5-10 minutes
Respond to God by telling Him how you feel about what you sensed or didn't sense during this meditation. If you need to present questions to God, do so.

❶ After allowing a few minutes for private prayer, ask group members to pray for the person on their left. Anyone wishing to pray silently may do so by saying, "I'm praying silently," then signifying when he or she is finished by saying "Amen."

Daily Lectio
If you wish, use the above format to meditate on God's Word between group meetings. You may wish to focus on today's passage every day this week, or you can use the following passages:

- Psalm 43:1-5 (asking God for light and truth in the midst of mourning)
- Isaiah 57:15-19 (from anger to healing)
- Jeremiah 31:7-13 (a prediction of how God would turn Judah's mourning into gladness)
- Luke 8:49-56 (Jesus heals Jairus's daughter)
- James 4:7-10 (instructions for those who mourn)
- Revelation 21:2-7 (when there will be no more mourning, crying, or pain)

---

1. Jan Johnson, *Enjoying the Presence of God* (Colorado Springs, Colo.: NavPress, 1996), pp. 112-113.

Jesus Speaks to the Caregivers' Heart

Mark 9:14-27

❶ After group members have had a chance to greet each other, read the centering instructions in the "Warming Up" section, then present the question and let the group members reflect quietly for a few minutes. Repeat the question and ask them to share their thoughts in a sentence or two. Anyone who wishes to pass may do so.

Warming Up   5-10 minutes

Center yourself by breathing in and out several times. Relax your neck and move it around. Then take time to relax the rest of your body. Turn each distraction over to God and set it aside. Ask yourself the following question to focus your thoughts for meditation on today's passage: How have I reacted to my experiences of caregiving (to a child, a younger sibling, an aging relative, an injured spouse)? Check as many boxes as are appropriate.

☐ I sensed God's comfort at times.
☐ It was draining.
☐ It encroached on my life.
☐ It made me cry at times.
☐ It felt like God's work at times.
☐ Other:

Reading the Passage   15-20 minutes

Read the following passage silently, noting the explanations in the shaded box.

❶ Ask a group member to read the passage aloud. Suggest that other group members close their eyes as they listen.

Mark 9:14-27

THE ARGUING ONLOOKERS

[14]When *they* came to the other disciples, they saw a large crowd around them and the *teachers of the Law* arguing with them. [15]As soon as all the people saw Jesus, they were overwhelmed with wonder and ran to greet him. [16]"What are you arguing with them about?" he asked.

THE FATHER CAREGIVER

[17]A man in the crowd answered, "Teacher, I brought you my son, who is *possessed by a spirit* that has robbed him of speech. [18]Whenever it seizes him, it throws him to the ground. He foams at the mouth, gnashes his teeth and becomes rigid. I asked your disciples to drive out the spirit, but they could not."

[19]"O *unbelieving generation,*" Jesus replied, "how long shall I stay with you? How long shall I put up with you? Bring the boy to me."

[20]So they brought him. When the spirit saw Jesus, it immediately threw the boy into a convulsion. He fell to the ground and rolled around, foaming at the mouth.

[21]Jesus asked the boy's father, "How long has he been like this?"

"From childhood," he answered. [22]"It has often thrown him into fire or water to kill him. But if you can do anything, take pity on us and help us."

[23]"'If you can'?" said Jesus. "Everything is possible for him who believes."

[24]Immediately the boy's father exclaimed, "I do believe; help me overcome my unbelief!"

THE HEALED SON

[25]When Jesus saw that a crowd was running to the scene, he rebuked the evil spirit. "You deaf and mute spirit," he said, "I command you, come out of him and never enter him again."

They — Jesus, Peter, James, and John were just returning from the place of Jesus' transfiguration.

Teachers of the Law — The scribes had tried to discredit Jesus, and now they had His disciples in an uproar, unable to show Jesus' authority and power as the Son of God.

Possessed by a spirit — A spirit from the enemy controlled this boy's actions, giving him symptoms similar to epilepsy.

Unbelieving generation — Jesus was often disappointed and exasperated at the lack of faith and hardness of heart of the disciples (Mark 4:40; 6:50,52; 8:17-21), who had already cast out demons successfully (Mark 6:13).

26The spirit shrieked, convulsed him violently and came out. The boy looked so much like a corpse that many said, "He's dead." 27But Jesus took him by the hand and lifted him to his feet, and he stood up.

If you haven't read the notes in the shaded box, read them now. Take a minute to consider the following questions.

❶ After reading the passage, ask group members to read the explanations in the shaded box and jot down answers to the questions below. After a few minutes, have them choose one question and share their answer in a sentence or two. Anyone who wishes to pass may do so. Explain that this is not a time for discussion but for reporting responses to the questions.

Jesus and the Boy's Father

1. Jesus engaged the father in conversation (verse 21), showing concern for the caregiver as well as the possessed boy. When, as a caregiver (to a child, a younger sibling, an aging relative, an injured spouse), would it have helped if someone had shown concern for you?

2. How does Jesus respond to the father's admission of his doubts?

THE FATHER ADMITS DOUBTS	JESUS' RESPONSE
"*If you can do anything,* take pity on us and help us." verse 22	
"I do believe; *help me overcome my unbelief!*" verse 24	

3. The father expressed both doubt and belief (verse 24). About what sorts of things do you have both faith and doubt?

☐ world crises
☐ family conflicts
☐ certain passages of Scripture
☐ certain doctrines in churches I've attended
☐ how God views controversial social issues
☐ other:

Jesus and the Others

4. Look at how frustrated Jesus seemed to be with the disciples (and perhaps the crowd and the teachers of the Law): "'O unbelieving generation,' Jesus replied,

'how long shall I stay with you? How long shall I put up with you? Bring the boy to me.'" (verse 19). He reproved them while He offered reassurance to the ambivalent father. Ponder why Jesus treated these people so differently.

5. Which of these tasks do you find daunting? Why do you find them daunting? (Check as many boxes as you wish.)

☐ being a "healer" like the disciples and needing to have faith
☐ being a caregiver like the father and needing to find help from God
☐ being a needy person like the boy, needing to accept Jesus' hand to get up

Picturing the Passage   10-15 minutes
Before reading the passage again, consider these cues.

Character Cue: The Boy's Condition
Scripture provides this picture of the boy:

■ dusty, with a dirt-streaked face from the foam at his mouth (verse 20)
■ may have had burn marks on his body because the demon had been throwing him into fires since he was a child (verse 22)
■ probably bore the marks of battering from convulsions and being thrown into water, where he may have fallen on rocks (verses 20,22)
■ startled by the noise of the crowd and by his own voice after so many years of being deaf and mute (verse 25)

Cultural Cue: The Teachers of the Law
The teachers of the Law (or scribes) were not necessarily Pharisees, although they generally appeared together. Pharisees were members of a political party, but teachers of the Law were judges in the religious tribunals. They had status and held an office. They were generally regarded as the mouthpiece and representative of the people, posing questions, urging objections, expecting explanations and respectful behaviors.[1]

Setting Cue: The Remoteness of the Location
About this time, Jesus was traveling around the Sea of Galilee, in and out of Jewish territory. He was far from Jewish "headquarters" (Jerusalem), but the teachers of the Law were present. This indicates their keen interest in Jesus, of which He was very aware.

Before reading the passage, consider which of the following viewpoints you might picture it from (you can choose more than one viewpoint):

- *the teachers of the Law* (Your primary interest is orthodoxy, and you're concerned about this upstart preacher, Jesus, who doesn't do things the conventional way of the Pharisees.)
- *the disciples* (Your primary interest is casting out a demon, which you have seen Jesus do many times [Mark 1:34,39; 5:15; 7:30; Matthew 9:33; 12:22; Luke 4:35; 8:2]. You may even be frustrated. After all, Jesus commanded you to drive out demons [Matthew 10:8], and He gave you authority to do so [Mark 3:15].)
- *the father of the demon-possessed boy* (You want your son healed. You have endured the demon's torture of him for a long time.)
- *the boy* (You have lived a noiseless life [at least since childhood]. You have been battered and burned. Other people talk to each other, but you have no part in this.)

Now read the passage aloud and close your eyes, picturing the events from one or more viewpoints, as if they were a movie playing in your mind.

❶ Have group members read these cues silently. Then ask a group member to read the passage aloud while the others picture the events.

Soaking In the Passage   5-15 minutes
To consider how this passage touches your life today, read it aloud again and ponder the following question for several minutes: *What word, phrase, special moment, or scene emerges from the passage and stays with me?*

After a few minutes, write the word, phrase, moment, or scene that resonates within you from the passage. Or, if you like, draw or doodle an abstract image or visual image in the margin of the page.

Word or phrase:

Moment or scene: I hear . . . I see . . .

❶ Have a different group member read the Scripture passage aloud and then state the question printed in italics. Have the group sit quietly together and fill in one of the blanks. After a few minutes, ask group members to read what they've written or show what they've drawn. Anyone who wishes to pass may do so.

Pondering the Invitation   5-15 minutes

Perhaps God is offering you an invitation in this passage to do or be something within the next few days. What might that be? Rest in the silence for a few minutes, pondering this question: *What do I sense this passage calling me to do or be right now?* This might involve a community position, a relationship with a friend or family member, a career move, or a change in your spiritual life. If nothing comes to mind, that's fine. Watch for insights in the next few days, but for now, simply sit in the quiet and enjoy God's presence.

❶ Read the instructions aloud and repeat the question printed in italics. Ask group members to respond by saying, "I sense this passage calling me to. . . ." Then complete that statement with a short phrase. Anyone who wishes to pass may do so.

Praying   5-10 minutes

Take a few minutes to respond to God about this meditation time. How do you feel about what you sensed (or didn't sense)? What do you most want to say to God at this time?

❶ After allowing a few minutes for private prayer, ask group members to pray for the person on their left. Anyone wishing to pray silently may do so by saying, "I'm praying silently," then signifying when he or she is finished by saying "Amen."

Daily Lectio

If you wish, use the above format to meditate on God's Word between group meetings. You may wish to focus on today's passage every day this week, or you can use the following passages:

- Psalm 86:11-15 (how God is compassionate and gracious, slow to anger, abounding in love and faithfulness)
- Psalm 112:1-6 (the interweaving of compassion and righteousness)
- Psalm 119:75-81 (asking for God's love, compassion, and protection)
- Luke 7:1-10 (Jesus heals a servant of a centurion, a caregiver of sorts)
- Luke 7:11-16 (Jesus raises a widow's son from the dead)
- John 4:46-54 (Jesus heals a son of a royal official)

---

1. Alfred Edersheim, *The Life and Times of Jesus the Messiah* (CITY?: Hendrickson Publishers, 1993), p. 65.

PART FOUR

HAVING THE HEART OF CHRIST

When God Calls You to Be Different
from Others

The Sanctified Imagination

Studying the Bible imparts information, which provides fuel for meditation, which changes the way we see. This, in turn, changes who we are and how we behave. Why? "The eyes of your heart [have been] enlightened" to see heaven's hope and inheritance (Ephesians 1:17-18). Through these enlightened eyes, we can learn to "fix our eyes not on what is seen, but on what is unseen" (2 Corinthians 4:18).

Other than in these two passages, the Bible doesn't say much about imagination except that it's a source of false prophecy and idol worship (Isaiah 65:2, Ezekiel 13:2). The truth about the imagination is that it is a force full of potential for either good or ill: "imagination lodges in the innermost part of our being where its potential for evil intentions or foolish ideas is laid bare by the piercing discernment of God's Word (Hebrews 4:12). What if imagination's potential for misleading us were reconfigured by the mind of Christ, which Paul claims we possess (1 Corinthians 2:16)? Armed, as was Christ's mind with stories, images, and hopes drawn from God's history with the people of God, imagination can become a penetrating force."[1]

Spiritual formation occurs as every part of ourselves becomes retrained and purified to obey Christ—tongue, thoughts, heart, feet, lips, arms, and knees (1 Peter 3:10, 2 Corinthians 10:5, James 4:8, Ephesians 6:15, Colossians 3:8, Hebrews 12:12)—and even the imagination. Jesus valued the human imagination and asked listeners to imagine buried treasure, an unjust judge, a mugging on the Jericho road, a house built on the sand, and someone fussing over having a tiny gnat in his drink but not even noticing the camel sitting in it. In parables, images, and word pictures, Jesus stimulated listeners' imaginations. For too long, we've let our imaginations be hijacked by lesser forces. As Christ's present-day listeners, it's our responsibility to respond to Him and let our imaginations be retrained for His purposes.

---

1. John Mogabgab, editor's introduction, *Weavings* 12 (Jan/Feb 1997): 2-3.

Vulnerable Enough to Serve
John 13:1-7,12-15

Warming Up 5-10 minutes

Before answering the question below, reflect quietly for at least two minutes. To help center yourself, try the following:

- Breathe in and out deeply five or six times. Relax your neck and move it around. Let your arms go limp and relax your legs and ankles. Relax each part from the inside out.
- Use the "palms down, palms up" method to turn your distractions over to God. Rest your hands in your lap, placing the palms down whenever you think of concerns you need to turn over to God. Turn your palms up as a symbol of your desire to receive from the Lord and set aside distractions.

Quietly move into a different position for a few minutes. Find a chair and face it. Get down on your hands and knees as if you were scrubbing someone's floor. Then look up at the empty chair and ponder what it would be like to carry on a conversation with a person sitting in the chair. It is that person's floor you are scrubbing. What would it be like to look up continually to that person and care for his or her floor?

Then move back to your normal place of meditation, close your eyes and consider this quiet question: Whose floor would you be willing to scrub, especially if that person were standing over you? Whose floor would it be difficult to scrub?

---

❶ After your group has had a chance to greet each other, ask half to be seated and ask the other half to find a place on the floor in front of one of the seated group members. Ask those on the floor to get on their hands and knees as if they were scrubbing the floor of the person in front of them. The seated group members should then give instructions regarding the toughest spots on the floor to clean (they can make this up).

After two or three minutes, ask seated persons and floor scrubbers to switch places and do the same. After another two or three minutes, ask everyone to take their seats, close their eyes and quiet themselves. Then state the above quiet questions. Give group members a couple of minutes to ponder this. Then ask them to share their answer in a sentence or two. Anyone who wishes to pass may do so.

Reading the Passage

If you have read the passage about the foot washing before, set aside ideas you've associated with it. Read the passage silently and then read the explanations in the shaded box.

> ❶ Ask a group member to read the Scripture passage aloud. Suggest that other group members close their eyes as they listen.

John 13:1-7,12-15

THE SETTING

[1]It was just before the Passover Feast. Jesus knew that the time had come for him to *leave this world* and go to the Father. Having loved his own who were in the world, he now showed them the *full extent of his love.* [2]The evening meal was being served, and the devil had already prompted Judas Iscariot, son of Simon, to betray Jesus. [3]Jesus knew that the Father had put all things under his power, and that he had come from God and was returning to God;

THE EXAMPLE

[4]so he got up from the meal, took off his outer clothing, and wrapped a towel around his waist. [5]After that, he poured water into a basin and began to *wash his disciples' feet,* drying them with the towel that was wrapped around him.

[6]*He came to Simon Peter,* who said to him, "Lord, are you going to wash my feet?" [7]

Jesus replied, "You do not realize now what I am doing, but later you will understand." . . .

Leave this world—The events in John 12:1–19:18 describe the final week of Jesus' life before His crucifixion.

Full extent of his love—Before their death, people often want to express the full extent of their love to those closest to them.

Wash his disciples' feet—Feet were the primary means of transportation in biblical times and they got dirty and injured because people wore sandals most of the time. Consider how well we would wash the tires of our cars if they customarily rolled into the living areas of our homes and rested under the covers in our beds.

He came to Simon Peter—Imagine Peter watching Jesus move around the group washing feet and finally stopping before him. How could his leader do this degrading task? William Barclay says, "The disciples of the Rabbis were supposed to render their masters' personal service, but a service like this would never have been dreamed of."[1]

THE TEACHING

[12]When he had finished washing their feet, he put on his clothes and returned to his place. "Do you understand what I have done for you?" he asked them. [13]"You call me 'Teacher' and 'Lord,' and rightly so, for that is what I am. [14]Now that I, your Lord and Teacher, have washed your feet, you also should wash one another's feet. [15]I have set you an example that you should do as I have done for you."

If you haven't read the notes in the shaded box, read them silently now. Take a minute to consider the following questions.

> ❶ After reading the passage, ask group members to read the explanations in the shaded box and then jot down answers to the questions below. After a few minutes, ask them to choose one question and share their answer in a sentence or two. Anyone who wishes to pass may do so. Explain that this is not a time for discussion but for reporting responses to the questions.

Vulnerability

1. Jesus' service becomes especially meaningful in light of what the devil was prompting Judas to do (verse 2).

   - Jesus was not just in safe territory, but the Enemy's forces were present.
   - Jesus served this false friend who planned to betray Him the same way He served His true friends.

   Can you think of a time when you served an enemy? If so, when? What was it like?

2. Jesus showed physical signs of vulnerability by:

   - sitting at other people's feet
   - taking off outer clothes
   - doing the work of a slave

   The closest thing to a reason Jesus offered for His vulnerability appears in verse 3: "Jesus knew that the Father had put all things under his power, and that he had come from God and was returning to God." Jesus knew who He was — how does that help us with humility?

3. The problem with vulnerability is that it makes us feel as if we have no defense against people who aren't concerned for our best interest. Being vulnerable to others doesn't mean we forget about our own needs, but that we present them to God (and sometimes to others) so that together we can figure out how to get those needs met.

Sometimes God prompts us to serve people, but we ignore Him because we're afraid we won't get certain needs met. When you find yourself unwilling to call someone or mow his or her lawn or invite him or her into your home, which of the following needs are you most concerned about?

☐ my need to get a word in edgewise
☐ my need to be respected
☐ my need for time to fulfill responsibilities
☐ my need for rest and leisure
☐ my need for time alone
☐ other:
☐ other:
☐ other:

4. How do you respond to Jesus' challenge to attempt this sort of vulnerable service? Check as many boxes as you like. Jesus' challenge to be vulnerable is . . .

☐ scary
☐ threatening, requires too much risk
☐ objectionable
☐ beyond my faith
☐ too much work
☐ something I want to try more of
☐ interesting; I'd like to try it out
☐ intriguing; I'm not sure how this could be true: "Now that you know these things, you will be blessed if you do them" (verse 17)

If any of the above questions are too difficult, hold them before God for a few minutes and then go on. Don't worry about getting an answer, but be open to what may come to you in the next few days.

Picturing the Passage   10-15 minutes
Before reading the passage again, consider these cues. Let them help you set the scene of how this event in Scripture might have occurred.

Cultural Cue: The Inner Garment
Men wore an inner garment close to the skin, usually made of linen or wool. Teachers often wore it down to the feet. This was probably what Jesus wore as He washed the disciples' feet. That means He stood there and took off His outer garment, wrapped at the waist with a wide cloth or leather belt, called a girdle. He also would have taken off His *tallith*—a rectangular or square outer garment teachers wore over the top of the body.[2]

Cultural Cue: Foot Washing
The roads of Palestine were not paved. In dry weather, they were inches deep in dust; in wet weather, they were liquid mud. Sandals were nothing more than soles

with a few straps. Great water pots were set at the door of most homes, and a servant washed the feet of guests as they came in.

Character Cue: Jesus as a Leader

Jesus' company of friends had no servants, and no one in this competitive bunch (Matthew 20:20-28) had taken the role of the servant. Jesus remedied this glaring omission by doing the work no one else would do—foot washing.

Now that you've looked at these cues, take a few minutes to read the passage again—aloud this time. Close your eyes, putting yourself in the place of one of the disciples. Hear the pots being moved and the water poured, and feel your feet being rubbed. Consider what you as a disciple might be thinking as Jesus moves around the group to you. What is it like to have the Son of God wash your feet (or scrub your floor, or clean your bathroom, if those images are more helpful)?

❶ Have group members read the cues silently. Then ask group members to put themselves in the place of one of the disciples as another group member reads the passage aloud.

Soaking In the Passage   5-15 minutes

Consider this all-important question that should be addressed whenever you read Scripture: How is my life touched by this passage today? Read the passage aloud again and ponder the following question for about five minutes: *What word, phrase, dramatic moment, touch, or sound emerges from the passage and stays with me?* If you begin to latch on to something that is most evident, step back a minute and wait to see if anything else emerges. Here are some examples of moments, scenes, or images:

- a feeling of confusion, even slight nausea or horror, when Jesus takes off His outer garment in front of the group, appearing as a slave, and begins washing feet
- a desire to understand when Jesus says, "Do you understand what I have done for you?" (verse 12)
- image: Jesus holding a towel, kneeling before you
- phrases (circle one): full extent of His love, come from God . . . returning to God; I, your Lord and Teacher, have washed your feet

After a few minutes, write about the word, phrase, or dramatic moment that resonates within you from the passage.

Word or phrase:

Moment: I hear . . . I see . . .

❶ Ask a different group member to read the passage aloud and then state the question printed in italics. Ask the group to sit quietly and then fill in one of the blanks above. After a few minutes, ask group members to read what they've written. Anyone who wishes to pass may do so.

Pondering the Invitation   5-15 minutes

Perhaps God is offering you an invitation in this passage to do or be something in the next few days. What might that be? Sit quietly for a while, pondering this question: *What do I sense this passage calling me to do or be right now?* If nothing comes, that's fine. Watch for insights in the next few days, but for now, simply sit in the quiet and enjoy God's presence.

❶ Read the above instructions aloud. After a few minutes, repeat the question printed in italics. Ask group members to respond by saying, "I sense this passage calling me to. . . ." Then complete that statement with a short phrase. Anyone who wishes to pass may do so. Encourage members to listen respectfully and prayerfully to other group members.

Praying   5-10 minutes

Take a few minutes to respond to God about all of this. How do you feel about what you sensed (or didn't sense)? What is it you most want to say to God at this time?

❶ After allowing a few minutes for private prayer, ask group members to pray for the person on their left. Anyone wishing to pray silently may do so by saying, "I'm praying silently," then signifying when he or she is finished by saying "Amen."

Daily Lectio

If you wish, use the above format to meditate on God's Word between group meetings. You may wish to focus on today's passage every day this week (try using a different version of the Bible besides NIV) or use the following passages:

- John 13:8-11 (a scene from today's passage not studied)
- John 15:20-27 (no servant is greater than his master)
- Romans 12:9-13 (being devoted to one another)
- Galatians 5:13-14 (serving one another in love)
- Ephesians 6:7-8 (serving wholeheartedly)
- Philippians 2:5-11 (Jesus extends His servanthood to the ultimate degree)

1. William Barclay, *The Daily Bible Study: The Gospel of John* vol. 2 (Philadelphia, Penn.: Westminster Press), p. 160.
2. Alfred Edersheim, *The Life and Times of Jesus the Messiah* (Hendrickson Publishers, 1993), p. 428.

Surrendering My Drivenness
Matthew 5:38-42, Mark 9:35-37

> ❶ After group members have had a chance to greet each other, read the centering instructions in the "Warming Up" section. Then present the quiet question and let them reflect quietly for a few minutes. Repeat the question and ask them to share their thoughts in a sentence or two. Anyone who wishes to pass may do so.

Warming Up   5-10 minutes

Center yourself by breathing in and out several times. Relax your neck and then take time to let your muscles relax. Turn over each distraction as you ask yourself the following question: In what ways might someone consider me a "loser"? Close your eyes and take a few minutes to quietly consider past experiences and relationships. Nothing may come to you until later, but let the process begin now.

Reading the Passages   15-20 minutes

Read the following passages, noting the explanations in the shaded box.

> ❶ Ask a group member to read the Scripture passages aloud. Suggest that other group members close their eyes as they listen.

Matthew 5:38-42

THE HEART WILLING TO GO THE EXTRA MILE

38"You have heard that it was said, *'Eye for eye, and tooth for tooth.'* 39But I tell you, *Do not resist an evil person.* If someone strikes you on the right cheek, turn to him the other also. 40And if someone wants to sue you and take your *tunic, let him have your cloak* as well. 41If someone *forces you to go one mile,* go with him two miles. 42Give to the one who asks you, and do not turn away from the one who wants to borrow from you."

Mark 9:35-37

THE HEART WILLING TO BE LAST

[35]Sitting down, Jesus called the Twelve and said, "If anyone wants to be first, he must be the very last, and the servant of all." [36]He took a little child and had him stand among them. Taking him in his arms, he said to them, [37]"Whoever welcomes one of *these little children* in my name welcomes me; and whoever welcomes me does not welcome me but the one who sent me."

If you haven't read the notes in the shaded box, read them now. Take a minute to consider the following questions.

❶ After reading the passages, ask group members to read the explanations in the shaded box and then jot down answers to the questions below. After a few minutes, have them choose one question and share their answer in a sentence or two. Anyone who wishes to pass may do so. Explain that this is not a time for discussion but for reporting responses to the questions.

Surrender
1. It's a monumental struggle to give up vying for what we want or what will advance our own cause. We fear what will happen if we surrender our will. Check the boxes below that describe the fears you sense within yourself. I fear that . . .

Eye for eye, and tooth for tooth—This command was originally given to limit retaliation (Exodus 21:23-25) because at that time a person's life might be taken for injuring another's sight. This law had nothing to do with personal revenge.

Do not resist an evil person—Christians do resist the Devil (James 4:7) and societal forces of evil (Ephesians 6:13), but they don't take personal revenge.[1]

Tunic . . . cloak—A tunic was the inner garment worn close to the skin, which could be held in pledge. A cloak (the outer garment usually worn with a belt or girdle) could not be held in pledge. It had to be returned, even to a poor person.

Forces you to go . . .—Roman soldiers could force others to carry their equipment for a mile.

These little children—Although our society is child-centered, children were second-class citizens in biblical times. Jesus spent a great deal of time welcoming insignificant people—including children.

☐ God, who "supplies all my needs," won't prevent me from being exploited.
☐ God won't meet my needs during the second mile.
☐ Life will be desolate during the second mile.
☐ I will lose too many material things in the process.
☐ Other:
☐ Other:

2. When we're asked to "give to him who asks you," we respond in several different ways:

■ give with a full heart
■ give grudgingly
■ try to pretend we didn't hear
■ rationalize why we can't be expected to consider the request
■ refuse to consider it as a possibility

   If we view this phrase as a command to give anything away that's asked of us, we have to whip our attitudes and actions into shape. If we view it as God telling us what kind of heart to have, we sense His invitation to go to Him and present our unwilling hearts for repair. Who do you know who has a willing, surrendered heart?

3. Consider this paraphrase of Mark 9:35 ("If anyone wants to be *first,* he must be the very *last,* and the servant of all," emphasis added): If anyone wants to be a *winner,* he must become a *loser.* The people who aren't bitter losers have a realistic sense of who they are. In what ways does knowing Christ give you a realistic sense of who you are?

☐ I can recognize and admit my mistakes better.
☐ I can feel accepted in spite of my mistakes.
☐ I feel hopeful about how God works in me.
☐ I can trust God to make up for the things I cannot do.
☐ I can trust God to lead me to do the things I need to do.
☐ Other:

4. Consider this paraphrase of Acts 20:35 ("It is more blessed to give than to receive"): "According to Jesus, it is more important to give justice and mercy than to receive it."[2] When we're wronged by someone—another driver, a corporation, a coworker—it's difficult to show justice and mercy rather than demand it from them. Have you ever offered justice and mercy instead of demanding it? Did you have good feelings about it? If so, what was involved in those good feelings?

☐ relief at not having to win
☐ freedom from having to be in control
☐ admiration of Christ for His ability to do this at all
☐ elation at not having to be right
☐ peace with not having to have the last word

☐ other:
☐ other:

5. These Scripture passages speak about vulnerability, as did the last session. They require a larger view of life and our place in God's world. We have to see ourselves in God's hands: "Jesus knew that the Father had put all things under his power, and that he had come from God and was returning to God" (John 13:3).

   If you wish, on page 130 draw a simple doodle that represents your belief that you are in God's hands (serious cartooning or artwork will take too much time), or draw a symbol of absolute dependence on God, using shapes or lines, such as this Chinese symbol for faith:

Picturing the Passages   10-15 minutes
Read the Scripture passages aloud this time and then close your eyes, putting yourself in one or all of these places:

   ■ walking unarmed into a violent situation to make peace
   ■ standing at the roadside, offering to carry a Roman soldier's equipment another mile
   ■ offering help to someone who has treated you badly

   If these images make you uncomfortable, try imagining yourself in God's hands as you do these things.

❶ Have group members read the suggestions and then ask them to put themselves in one of the situations as another group member reads the Scripture passages aloud.

Soaking In the Passages   5-15 minutes
Consider how your life is touched by these passages. Read the passages aloud again and ponder the following question for several minutes: *Is there within these passages a word or phrase that stays with me?* If you begin to latch on to something that is most evident, step back a minute and wait to see if anything else emerges.

   After several minutes, write a word or phrase that resonates with you from the passages.

   Word or phrase:

❶ Ask a different group member to read the Scripture passage aloud and then state the question printed in italics. Have the group sit quietly and fill in the blank when they're ready. After a few minutes, ask group members to read what they've written. Anyone who wishes to pass may do so.

Pondering the Invitation   5-15 minutes

Perhaps God is offering you an invitation in these Scripture passages to do or be something within the next few days. What might that be? Sit in silence for a few minutes, pondering this question: *What do I sense these passages calling me to do or be right now?* Be open to the quietness, but don't feel pressured to come up with an answer.

❶ Read the above instructions aloud. After a few minutes, repeat the question printed in italics. Ask group members to respond by saying, "I sense this passage calling me to. . . ." Then complete that statement with a short phrase. Anyone who wishes to pass may do so.

Praying   5-10 minutes

Take a few minutes to respond to God about these passages. How do you feel about what you sensed (or didn't sense)? What is it you most want to say to God at this time?

❶ After allowing a few minutes for private prayer, ask group members to pray for the person on their left. Anyone wishing to pray silently may do so by saying, "I'm praying silently," then signifying when he or she is finished by saying "Amen."

Daily Lectio

If you wish, use the above format to meditate on God's Word between group meetings. You may wish to focus on today's passages every day this week, or you can use the following passages:

- Psalm 18:25-32 (how God rescues the humble)
- Matthew 11:28-30 (God's yoke is easy and His burden is light)
- Ephesians 4:1-7 (a life worthy of our calling)
- James 4:7-10 (how submission to God is required to be humble with others)
- 1 Peter 3:8-16 (living together in harmony and peace)
- 1 Peter 5:6-10 (elements of humility)

---

1. *The Quest Study Bible* (Grand Rapids, Mich.: Zondervan, 1994), p. 1339.
2. *Life Application Bible* (Wheaton, Ill.: Tyndale House, 1991), p. 1656.

The Costs of Helping

Mark 1:35-45

❶ After group members have had a chance to greet each other, read the centering instructions in the "Warming Up" section. Then present the quiet question and let them reflect quietly for a few minutes. Repeat the question and ask them to share their thoughts in a sentence or two. Anyone who wishes to pass may do so.

Warming Up   5-10 minutes

Center yourself by breathing in and out several times. Relax your neck, then take time to let your muscles relax. Let go of distractions that pull you from focusing on God. Ask yourself the following quiet question to help focus your thoughts for meditation on today's passage: How has Christ been working in me recently?

Close your eyes and take a few minutes to consider the events of the week, conversations with people, and your thoughts to see if anything comes to you. If an answer to the above question doesn't come to you at this time, that's fine. Try to enjoy God's presence without having to do anything.

Reading the Passage   15-20 minutes

Read the following passage, noting the explanations in the shaded box.

❶ Ask a group member to read the Scripture passage aloud. Suggest that other group members close their eyes as they listen.

Mark 1:35-45

CARVING OUT TIME WITH GOD

³⁵Very early in the morning, while it was still dark, Jesus got up, left the house and went off to a solitary place, where he prayed. ³⁶Simon

and his companions went to look for him, [37]and when they found him, they exclaimed: "Everyone is looking for you!"

[38]Jesus replied, "Let us go somewhere else — to the nearby villages — so I can preach there also. That is why I have come." [39]So he traveled throughout Galilee, preaching in their synagogues and driving out demons.

THE WILLING, COMPASSIONATE HEART

[40]A man with *leprosy* came to him and begged him on his knees, "If you are willing, you can make me clean."

[41]Filled with compassion, Jesus reached out his hand and *touched* the man. "I am willing," he said. "Be clean!" [42]Immediately the leprosy left him and he was cured.

[43]Jesus sent him away at once with a strong warning: [44]"See that you *don't tell this to anyone*. But go, show yourself to the priest and offer the sacrifices that Moses commanded for your cleansing, as a testimony to them." [45]Instead he went out and began to talk freely, spreading the news. As a result, Jesus could no longer enter a town openly but *stayed outside in lonely places*. Yet the people still came to him from everywhere.

If you haven't read the notes in the shaded box, read them now. Take a minute to consider the following questions.

❶ After reading the Scripture passage, ask group members to read silently the explanations in the shaded box and then jot down answers to the questions below. After a few minutes, have them choose one question and share their answer in a sentence or two. Anyone who wishes to pass may do so. Explain that this is not a time for discussion but for reporting responses to the questions.

Leprosy — In biblical times, leprosy included several skin ailments, many of which were contagious and incurable. Some resulted in paralysis and gangrene.

Touched — Doctors, dentists, and nurses today wisely limit the extent of their physical contact by wearing gloves and masks. With lepers, caregivers were wise to avoid touch at all. Yet touch was an important part of Jesus' healings, no matter what the disease. Jesus seemed to know the need people had for human touch, and in His healings, He offered that "medicine" as well.

Don't tell this to anyone — Publicity of His miracles would bring Jesus unwanted attention from His opponents, the Jewish leaders. He needed to fulfill His mission of preaching and healing before He could allow them to capture Him.

Stayed outside in lonely places — Because the healed leper spread the news, Jesus' freedom was limited. Yet His compassion had moved Him to heal the man anyway.

Jesus' Getaways

1. Throughout the Gospels, Jesus escaped for long periods to pray. He must have enjoyed renewing the close fellowship with the Father to which He was accustomed (Matthew 14:23; Mark 1:35, 6:46; Luke 5:16, 6:12). Only in the Gethsemane prayers and the prayer in John 17 does Scripture say explicitly what Jesus prayed. What do you think Jesus might have talked about with His Father? (If you're familiar with biblical teaching on prayer, draw from that.)

Being "Sensible" About Compassion

2. Some would say Jesus didn't use common sense when He healed the leper. First of all, He endangered His own physical health by touching the man. Also, the publicity of the miracle made it difficult for Jesus to preach in towns and accomplish His mission on earth. Jesus foresaw this difficulty but healed the man anyway.

   What risks are involved when we respond in compassion to people?

3. We often have the so-called "common sense" not to touch a contagious person or invest time in someone who will cost us dearly. We may be moved with feelings of compassion, as Jesus was, but the thought occurs to us, *Yes, but look at the results.* How do you think God views your response to your feelings of compassion?

   ☐ too calculating
   ☐ too impulsive
   ☐ too insecure to do anything about my compassion
   ☐ other:

Picturing the Passage   10-15 minutes

Before reading the passage again, consider this cue.

Cultural Cue: Leprosy

Because leprosy was contagious and incurable, Old Testament law (Leviticus 13–14) did not allow lepers to participate in social and religious activities. Those who touched lepers were considered "unclean." Jews saw leprosy as a sign of God's curse and some threw rocks at lepers to keep them away. (Reread note on "leprosy" in the shaded box on page 132.)

   Imagine grasping the hand of someone with a repulsive skin disease. The nerves to his extremities have been long dead; his fingers are infected and rotting away from gangrene. The tips of his thumb and forefinger are completely gone. You can feel the running sores as you take the hand in yours. What feelings would this evoke in you? Imagine also what feelings this touch would evoke in the person. Keep in mind these two things as you imagine this:

- Jesus' touch was compassionate, not clinical or mechanical in nature.
- People who are not often touched for various reasons have what is called "skin hunger." They are "starved" for touch.

Armed with the above cue, read the Scripture passage aloud and then close your eyes, picturing the events as if they were a movie playing in your mind.

If you wish, ponder from the viewpoint of the leper. Consider the greatest handicap in your life: poor eyesight, pitted skin, arthritis, back pain, past fractures, migraine headaches, knees that go out on you. . . . What would it mean to you to be instantly rid of this problem (verse 42)? What would you say to the person who freed you from this?

❶ Have group members read the Cultural Cue and the instructions. Then have a group member read the Scripture passage aloud while the others picture the passage.

Soaking In the Passage   5-15 minutes
Reflect on how this passage speaks to you today. Read the passage aloud again and ponder the following question for several minutes: *What word, phrase, dramatic moment, or scene from the passage stays with me?*

After several minutes, write the word, phrase, images, or scenes that resonate within you from the Scripture passage. Write only a sentence or two.

Word or phrase:

Scene or image: I hear . . . I see . . .

❶ Ask a group member to read the passage aloud and then state the question printed in italics. Have the group sit quietly together for a while and then fill in one of the blanks above. After a few minutes, ask group members to read what they've written. Anyone who wishes to pass may do so.

Pondering the Invitation   5-15 minutes
Perhaps God is offering you an invitation in this passage to absorb truth about Him or to do or be something within the next few days. What might that be? Sit quietly for a few minutes, pondering these questions: *What do I need to know? What do I need to do? How do I need to change?*

❶ Read the above instructions aloud. After a few minutes, repeat the questions printed in italics. Ask group members to respond by saying, "I sense this passage calling me to. . . ." Then complete that statement with a short phrase. Anyone who wishes to pass may do so.

Praying   5-10 minutes

Take a few minutes to respond to God about this meditation. How do you feel about what you sensed (or didn't sense)? What is it you most want to say to God at this time?

❶ After allowing a few minutes for private prayer, ask group members to pray for the person on their left. Anyone wishing to pray silently may do so by saying, "I'm praying silently," then signifying when he or she is finished by saying "Amen."

Daily Lectio

If you wish, use the above format to meditate on God's Word between group meetings. You may wish to focus on today's passage every day this week or you can use the following passages:

- Psalm 103:1-12 (God's compassion)
- Psalm 103:13-22 (praise for the compassionate God)
- Psalm 145:1-9 (praising God for His compassion)
- Mark 8:22-25 (Jesus heals a blind man, using touch in a creative way)
- Luke 6:17-19 (Jesus heals a crowd of people)
- Luke 18:15-17 (people wanting Jesus to bless and touch their babies)

Responding to My Opponents

Matthew 5:43-48, Luke 6:36

❶ After group members have had a chance to greet each other, read the prayer in the "Warming Up" section. Let group members reflect quietly for a few more minutes and then ask them to say aloud the word or words from the prayer that resonate most within them. (If you wish, read the prayer again.) Anyone who wishes to pass may do so.

Warming Up   5-10 minutes

After you center yourself and set aside distractions, read aloud the prayer that follows and reflect in the quiet. If you wish, read it aloud again.

Lord, make me an instrument of your peace. Where there is hatred, let me sow love; where there is injury, pardon; where there is doubt, faith; where there is despair, hope; where there is darkness, light; and where there is sadness, joy.

O divine Master, grant that I may not so much seek to be consoled as to console; to be understood as to understand; to be loved as to love. For it is in giving that we receive; it is in pardoning that we are pardoned; and it is in dying that we are born to eternal life.[1]

Reading the Passage   15-20 minutes

As you read this familiar passage of Scripture, try to hear it with fresh ears. Read the explanations in the shaded box.

❶ Ask a group member to read the Scripture passage aloud. Suggest that other group members close their eyes as they listen.

Matthew 5:43-48, Luke 6:36

A RADICAL COMMAND

⁴³"You have heard that it was said, 'Love your neighbor and hate your enemy.' ⁴⁴But I tell you: *Love* your enemies and pray for those who persecute you, ⁴⁵that you may be sons of your Father in heaven. He causes His sun to rise on the evil and the good, and sends rain on the righteous and the unrighteous. ⁴⁶If you love those who love you, what reward will you get? Are not even the tax collectors doing that? ⁴⁷And if you greet only your brothers, what are you doing more than others? Do not even pagans do that?

MATTHEW 5:48

Be *perfect*, therefore, as your heavenly Father is perfect.

LUKE 6: 36

Be merciful, just as your Father is merciful.

Matthew 5:43-48 and Luke 6:27-36 are parallel passages. Luke 6:36 and Matthew 5:45 are the only verses that use significantly different Greek words and is translated differently. This idea was a life-message for Jesus and He probably preached it in many different ways at many different times.

If you haven't read the notes in the shaded box, read them silently now. Take a minute to consider the following questions.

❶ After the passage is read, ask group members to read the explanations in the shaded box and jot down answers to the questions below. After a few minutes, have them choose one question and share their answer in a sentence or two. Anyone who wishes to pass may do so. Explain that this is not a time for discussion but for reporting responses to the questions.

"Your Enemies"

1. The first hearers of these words were probably appalled at the thought of loving their Roman oppressors. You may not have a political oppressor, but you probably have other "enemies." Consider for a moment who those people are. Write their initials after the following descriptions.

Love —Love involves respecting someone, being kind to him, and meeting his needs as you are able. This doesn't require affection, but it does help to have a heart for that person.

Perfect —The original Greek word implies completion and maturity. Love completes the Law, which is why Jesus said that the Law and the prophets hang on these two commandments: to love God and love your neighbor (Matthew 22:37-40). These are a mature expression of the Law.

- People you avoid:
- People you find difficult to deal with:
- People who treat you disrespectfully:
- People who don't like you:

2. These verses beg us to consider the humanity of those who have been unjust, and possibly inhumane, to us. One practical way to do this is to pray for them. Here are some prayers to offer regarding your enemies. Add a few more prayers, if possible.

- God, show me the heart of this person.
- God, what does this person need from me?
- God, what does this person need from You?
- God, is there anything I can do to reconcile with this person?
- Other:

3. Here are a few examples of how Jesus showed love to His enemies.

JESUS AND HIS ENEMIES	HOW JESUS SHOWED LOVE
During Jesus' arrest, a disciple struck the servant of the high priest, cutting off his right ear. (Luke 22:50-52)	touched the "enemy's" ear and healed him
At the crucifixion, Jesus forgave His executioners on the spot, not holding their deeds against them. (Luke 23:34)	forgave enemies and accepted the circumstances as part of God's larger picture
At the request of the legion of demons, Jesus put them into swine instead of into the Abyss. (Luke 8:26-39)	lightened the consequences of His enemies
Jesus indicates His desire to gather the unbelieving Jews to Himself. (Matthew 23:37-39; Luke 19:41-44)	grieved for the consequences that His enemies would suffer

Which of these examples in the right-hand column fascinates you most? Why?

Picturing the Passage   10-15 minutes

Choose one of these images to represent the "enemy" as you picture the Scripture passage:

- take the view of the Jews: picture the Romans or Samaritans or any foreign nation
- take the view of the disciples: picture the Pharisees
- take a personal view and use the face of someone whom you find difficult

Now read the passage aloud this time, and then close your eyes, picturing yourself as one of the radically different "children of your Father in heaven" (verse 45, NRSV).

> ❶ Ask group members to read the instructions above and allow them time to choose their image of an enemy. Ask one person to read the passage aloud as the others picture the passage.

Soaking In the Passage   5-15 minutes

Consider how these Scripture verses touch your life today. Read the passage aloud again and ponder the following question for several minutes: *What word, phrase, scene, or moment emerges from the passage and stays with me?* If you begin to latch on to something that is most evident, set it aside for a minute and wait to see if anything else emerges.

After several minutes, write the word or image that resonates from the passage.

Word or phrase:

Scene: I hear . . . I see . . .

> ❶ Ask a group member to read the passage aloud and then state the question printed in italics. Ask group members to sit quietly and then fill in one of the blanks above. After a few minutes, ask group members to read what they've written. Anyone who wishes to pass may do so.

Pondering the Invitation   5-15 minutes

Perhaps God is offering you an invitation in this passage to do or be something within the next few days. What might that be? Reflect quietly for several minutes, pondering this question: *What do I sense this passage calling me to do or be right now?* If nothing comes to mind, that's fine. Watch for insights in the next few days, but for now, simply sit in the quiet and enjoy God's presence.

❶ Read the instructions aloud in the "Pondering the Invitation" section. After a few minutes, repeat the question printed in italics. Ask group members to respond by saying, "I sense this passage calling me to. . . ." Then complete that statement with a short phrase. Anyone who wishes to pass may do so.

Praying   5-10 minutes

Take a few minutes to respond to God about these ideas. How do you feel about what you sensed (or didn't sense)? What is it you most want to say to God at this time?

❶ After allowing a few minutes for private prayer, ask group members to pray for the person on their left. Anyone wishing to pray silently may do so by saying, "I'm praying silently," then signifying when he or she is finished by saying "Amen."

Daily Lectio

If you wish, use the above format to meditate on God's Word between group meetings. You may wish to focus on today's passage every day this week, or you can use the following passages:

- John 5:16-20 (the Pharisees persecuting Jesus)
- Acts 11:19-21 (persecution of the church; the Lord's hand on the church)
- Romans 8:31-37 (neither persecution nor anything else can separate us from God's love)
- Romans 12:9-15 (sincere love means blessing those who persecute you)
- Romans 12:16-21 (feeding a hungry enemy)
- James 4:11-12 (setting aside slander and judgment)

---

1. Saint Francis of Assisi, as quoted in Veronica Zundel (Grand Rapids, Mich.: Eerdmans, 1983), p. 30.

Caring for the Forgotten

Luke 8:26-39, Mark 5:4-5

❶ After group members have had a chance to greet each other, read the information in the "Warming Up" section. Then present the question and let them reflect on it for a few minutes. Repeat the question and ask them to share their thoughts in a sentence or two. Anyone who wishes to pass may do so.

Warming Up   5-10 minutes

After quieting yourself and setting aside distractions, read the following story and use the quiet question to focus your thoughts for today's meditation.

In the book *Les Misérables,* the main character, Jean Valjean, was caught stealing silver plates from a bishop. When the police brought him back to the bishop, the bishop insisted that he had given them to Jean Valjean, and he heaped on him the silver candlesticks as well.

In a low voice, the bishop said to Valjean, "It is your soul that I am buying for you. I withdraw it from dark thoughts and from the spirit of perdition, and I give it to God."[1] Jean Valjean went on to become an extremely honest and selfless person.

Ponder this question quietly: What would it mean to give someone back his life?

Reading the Passage   15-20 minutes

Read the following Scripture passage, noting the explanations in the shaded boxes at the bottom of pages 144-145.

❶ Ask a group member to read the Scripture passage aloud. Suggest that other group members close their eyes as they listen.

Luke 8:26-29, Mark 5:4-5

"BEFORE"

26They sailed to the region of *the Gerasenes,* which is across the lake from Galilee. 27When Jesus stepped ashore, he was met by a *demon-possessed man* from the town. For a long time this man had not worn clothes or lived in a house, but had lived in the *tombs.* 28When he saw Jesus, he cried out and fell at his feet, shouting at the top of his voice, "What do you want with me, Jesus, Son of the Most High God? I beg you, don't torture me!" 29For Jesus had commanded the evil spirit to come out of the man. Many times it had seized him, and though he was chained hand and foot and kept under guard, he had broken his chains and had been driven by the demon into solitary places.

Mark 5:4-5

4*No one was strong enough to subdue him.* 5Night and day among the tombs and in the hills he would cry out and cut himself with stones.

Luke 8:30-39

THE DRAMATIC RESCUE

30 Jesus asked him, "What is your name?"

"Legion," he replied, because many demons had gone into him. 31And they begged him repeatedly not to order them to go into *the Abyss.* 32A large herd of pigs was feeding there on the hillside. The demons begged Jesus to let them go into them, and he gave them permission. 33When the demons came out of the man, they went into the

---

The Gerasenes — This Gentile region southeast of the Sea of Galilee, also known as the Gadarene region, included ten self-governing cities (Decapolis), was settled centuries earlier by Greek traders and immigrants. Many people from there followed Jesus (Matthew 4:25). The shore would have been green hilly country in the summer and chilly in the winter.

Demon-possessed man — Demons are evil spirits — beings with intelligence and personality — under Satan's control, working destruction on behalf of Satan. Whenever confronted by Jesus, they lost their power.

Tombs — These were probably hewn out of caves on the shore. Living in a graveyard made this man ceremonially unclean. (Of course, he already was because he was a Gentile and demon-possessed.) Influential teachers such as Jesus normally had no dealings with ceremonially unclean people.

No one was strong enough to subdue him — The account of this man is also given in Mark 5:1-20 and Matthew 8:28-34.

pigs, and the herd rushed down the steep bank into the lake and was drowned. ³⁴When those tending the pigs saw what had happened, they ran off and reported this in the town and countryside, ³⁵and the people went out to see what had happened.

"AFTER"

When they came to Jesus, they found the man from whom the demons had gone out, sitting at Jesus' feet, dressed and in his right mind; and they were afraid. ³⁶Those who had seen it told the people how the demon-possessed man had been cured. ³⁷Then all the people of the region of the Gerasenes asked Jesus to leave them, because they were overcome with fear. So he got into the boat and left.

³⁸The man from whom the demons had gone out begged to go with him, but Jesus sent him away, saying, ³⁹"Return home and tell how much God has done for you." So the man went away and told all over town how much Jesus had done for him.

    If you haven't read the notes in the shaded boxes, read them now. Take a minute to consider the following questions.

> ❶ After the passage is read, ask group members to read the explanations in the shaded boxes and jot down answers to the questions below. After a few minutes, have them choose one question and share their answer in a sentence or two. Anyone who wishes to pass may do so. Explain that this is not a time for discussion but for reporting responses to the questions.

Jesus' Compassion for This Demon-Possessed Man

1. The demon-possessed man was clearly a "throwaway" in first-century society, but Jesus often moved toward "throwaways": lepers, the blind and maimed, people with tattered reputations (Zacchaeus, Matthew, the woman taken in adultery, the woman at the well). How do you explain Jesus' ability to walk up to a man such as this and do what needed to be done and also show compassion for him?

Legion — The largest unit in the Roman army, having three thousand to six thousand soldiers.

The Abyss — The bottomless pit where Satan will be banished for a time before his ultimate destruction (Revelation 20:3).

2. In what situations do you need the clarity and compassion that Jesus had?

3. Jesus was not intimidated by evil and its various manifestations. He courageously dealt with a man you and I might hide from. Is there anyone you've met to whom you might compare this man? If so, how did you feel when you were around that person?

4. What do you think it was like to be around the demon-possessed man before he was healed? What was the noise level like? The odor? Check the boxes to indicate the range of emotional feelings, physical responses, and thoughts an observer might have had toward the man.

☐ revulsion at his appearance
☐ pity
☐ desire to run away
☐ fear of the man's unusual strength (could break chains)
☐ ears assaulted by the noise
☐ feeling sick to one's stomach
☐ trying not to look at his nakedness
☐ staring in a fascinated, morbid way at his wounds and filth
☐ comparing him to an animal
☐ giving him a pejorative nickname—Graveyard Goliath or Tombstone Tobiah
☐ wishing he would go back into the hills
☐ yelling at him to keep away
☐ resentment at taxpayers' money spent for constant guard and a supply of chains
☐ other:

Picturing the Passage   10-15 minutes
Before reading the passage again, consider these cues.

Character Cue: Jesus and Animals
Some people might find it difficult to meditate on this passage because Jesus' behavior seemed unfair to the owner of the pigs or the pigs themselves. The New Testament does not often record the death of so many animals, and its unusualness stands out.

Let's begin with what we know. Consider the apparent goal of Jesus: to heal the man and reconcile him to his community. But would the townspeople ever trust the man? Would they wonder if he was pretending to be sane so he could sneak up on them and attack them? Would they be tempted to keep him chained? Visible evidence of demon possession wasn't as obvious as that of physical healing, but the stampeding swine provided that helpful visual reminder to the man himself (who may have had his own doubts) and to his community.

As to why Jesus allowed the owner of the swine to pay a heavy financial burden for the man's healing (the cost of his livestock), we must rely on the promise that "the Lord is full of compassion and mercy" (James 5:11). In that light, the possibilities are endless. Was the swine owner the man's father? Was the owner a frequent tormentor of the man, touting him as the local crazy person? Was the owner a dealer in demonic forces whom Jesus wished to warn? Were the swine diseased and ready to be slaughtered, and perhaps Jesus did the owner a favor?

The stampeding swine were definitely a sign of mercy to the man and to the demons. This ended their destructive work within people. Unfamiliar with the realm of spirits as we are, we can caution ourselves not to judge harshly, but to trust.

Character Cue: The Man's Behavior and Appearance

Imagine how the possessed man looked before and after his dramatic rescue. Could he have had broken bones and lesions?

BEFORE	AFTER
for a long time this man had not worn clothes or lived in a house	dressed
lived in the tombs and in the hills	sitting at Jesus' feet
night and day he would cry out among the tombs	in his right mind
chained hand and foot	
kept under constant guard	
cut himself with stones	
many times [the demon] had seized him	
shouted at the top of his voice at Jesus	

Setting Cue: The Caves

About fifteen minutes south of Gersa on the Sea of Galilee shore is a steep bluff which descends abruptly on a narrow ledge of shore. The whole country around is burrowed with limestone caverns and rock chambers in which the local people buried their dead.[2] Try to picture one of these caves in your mind, one in which the demon-afflicted man had spent many a night. At the back of the cave lie the bones and decaying shrouds of several people who have been entombed there over the years. Nearer the front might be scraps of food and fishbones, the remnants of whatever the man has been living on. Might he have built fires occasionally, or did he simply endure the cold nights, seeking refuge in the cave when the wind blew chill off the lake? There is no bed, no lamp, no cloak—only rocks and bits of driftwood. There is no sound but the wind, the lapping of waves, and the cries of the demonized man.

Now that you've looked at these cues, take a few minutes to read the passage aloud this time. Then close your eyes and imagine yourself as one of the disciples standing on the seashore near the caves. Which is most difficult for you—courage or compassion? In what way does Jesus' behavior stun you the most?

> ❶ Have group members read these cues silently. Then have a group member read the passage aloud while the others picture the passage.

Soaking In the Passage   5-15 minutes

Consider how this scriptural account touches your life today. Read the passage aloud again and ponder the following question for several minutes: *What special moment, scene, image, sound, or smell emerges from the passage and stays with me?*

After several minutes, write about the images or words that resonate from the passage.

I hear . . . I see . . .

> ❶ Have a different group member read the passage aloud and then state the question printed in italics. Ask group members to sit quietly and then fill in the "I hear . . . I see" space. After a few minutes, ask group members to read what they've written. Anyone who wishes to pass may do so.

Pondering the Invitation   5-15 minutes

Perhaps God is offering you an invitation in this passage to do or be something within the next few days. What might that be? Sit quietly for several minutes, pondering this question: *What do I sense this passage calling me to do or be right now?* Let God speak to you beyond the first thing that comes to your mind. Perhaps this is about how you treat a specific person, or perhaps you are the wounded person. Perhaps you need courage to face a terrifying situation, or you're the one creating it. Don't pressure yourself to come up with an answer. Ask God, What do I need to know?

> ❶ Read the above instructions aloud, and after a few minutes, repeat the question printed in italics. Ask group members to respond by saying, "I sense this passage calling me to. . . ." Then complete that statement with a short phrase. Anyone who wishes to pass may do so.

Praying

Take a few minutes to respond to God about all of this. How do you feel about what you sensed (or didn't sense)? What is it you most want to say to God at this time?

> ❶ After allowing a few minutes for private prayer, ask group members to pray for the person on their left. Anyone wishing to pray silently may do so by saying, "I'm praying silently," then signifying when he or she is finished by saying "Amen."

Daily Lectio

If you wish, use the above format to meditate on God's Word between group meetings. You may wish to focus on today's passage every day this week, or you can use the following passages:

- Joel 2:12-13 (God's compassionate ways, beckoning people to return)
- Zechariah 7:8-10 (describing the need for a soft heart that shows compassion)
- Matthew 8:28-34 (parallel passage; how the story unfolds in a different gospel)
- Mark 5:1-20 (parallel passage; how the story unfolds in a different gospel)
- 1 Corinthians 16:13-14 (mixing compassion and courage)
- 2 Corinthians 1:3-7 (using God's compassion to comfort others)

---

1. Victor Hugo, *Les Misérables* (Greenwich, Conn.: Fawcett Publications, 1961), p. 39.
2. Edersheim, *The Life and Times of Jesus the Messiah* (MA: Hendrickson Publishers, 1993), pp. 418-419.

PART FIVE

BUILDING RELATIONSHIPS

When You'd Like to Connect Better
with Others

Is Quiet a Friend or an Enemy?

Being quiet in a group can be difficult. In groups, people talk! Group *lectio* provides a different kind of togetherness. You develop a sense of community without jabbering. When you're tempted to answer questions by rattling on and on, consider choosing fewer words. Offer only the words and images that resonate within you.

Don't be embarrassed if you're not sure what to say in a *lectio* group. *Lectio* asks you to look within, to take time to reflect before you speak, or to pass. You may do better doodling or drawing in the margin. If you're doing *lectio* by yourself and aren't sure how to respond, feel free to sing and walk or to lay facedown on the floor.

Once you get used to being quiet with God, silence can become a place of great struggle and great encounter. We can hear God soothe the voices in our minds that nag us about our past, about what we're supposed to do, about what others expect. We can respond from the truth of the passage: *Look at how God rescued the psalmist! Pushing myself forward doesn't lead to greatness.*

Once you're able to be with God in quiet moments, you may experience surprising feelings—sadness, anger, inadequacy, incompleteness, amusement, or surprise. You may even begin to cry over something you thought you were over. Ask yourself, *What's within me that needs to be brought to God—not erased or beaten down? What do I need to converse with Him about?* (If you're working in a group, admit these to the group if you possibly can.) If it's too intense to continue, write about it in the blank spaces of the book or draw a silly cartoon of yourself. Continue meditating. God will speak to you in a way that isn't too intense for you.

Jesus Responds to Failures
John 21:4-6,7,9,12,13-17

❶ After your group has had a chance to greet each other, read the centering instructions in the "Warming Up" section. Then ask the quiet question. Sit quietly for about two minutes, repeat the question, and ask group members to share their thoughts in a sentence or two. Anyone who wishes to pass may do so. After group members share, thank them and comment that it's helpful to hear the variety of ways God speaks to people.

Warming Up   5-10 minutes

Before beginning this meditation, reflect quietly for a few minutes. Breathe deeply and exhale five or six times. Relax your neck and move it around. Then let your arms go limp and relax your legs and ankles. Relax each part from the inside out.

If you have trouble quieting yourself, try using the "palms down, palms up" method. Rest your hands in your lap, placing the palms down whenever you think of concerns you need to turn over to God. Turn your palms up as a symbol of your desire to receive from the Lord and set aside distractions.

Consider this quiet question: What draws you to a group/individual study like this? Close your eyes and reflect on your past experiences or the pressing needs in your life right now. If an answer doesn't come to you at this time, that's fine. Try to enjoy God's presence without having to do anything.

Reading the Passage   15-20 minutes

Read the following passage, noting the explanations in the shaded box.

❶ Ask a group member to read the Scripture passage aloud. Suggest that other group members close their eyes as they listen.

John 21:4-6,7,9,12,13-17

THE DISCIPLES SEE JESUS

⁴Early in the morning, Jesus stood on the *shore,* but *the disciples* did not realize that it was Jesus.

⁵He called out to them, "Friends, haven't you any fish?"

"No," they answered.

⁶He said, "Throw your net on the right side of the boat and you will find some." When they did, they were unable to haul the net in because of the large number of fish.

JESUS SERVES BREAKFAST

⁷As soon as *Simon Peter* heard [John] say, "It is the Lord," he wrapped his outer garment around him (for he had taken it off) and jumped into the water. ⁹When they landed, they saw a fire of burning coals there with fish on it, and some bread.

¹²Jesus said to them, "Come and have breakfast." ¹³Jesus came, took the bread and gave it to them, and did the same with the fish. ¹⁴This was now the third time Jesus appeared to his disciples *after he was raised from the dead.*

JESUS AND PETER CONVERSE

¹⁵When they had finished eating, Jesus said to Simon Peter, "Simon son of John, do you truly love me more than these?"

"Yes, Lord," he said, "you know that I love you."

Jesus said, *"Feed my lambs."*

¹⁶Again Jesus said, "Simon son of John, do you truly love me?"

He answered, "Yes, Lord, you know that I love you."

Jesus said, "Take care of my sheep."

¹⁷The third time he said to him, "Simon son of John, do you love me?"

Shore—The Sea of Galilee, a large lake about seven-and-a-half miles across and thirteen miles long. The disciples had seen the resurrected Christ in Jerusalem but not in Galilee (sixty miles away).

The disciples—Peter, James, John, Thomas, Nathanael, and two others (21:1-3) had been fishing all night but caught nothing.

Simon Peter—Since the time Peter denied Jesus, they had not talked or seen each other except when Jesus appeared to the disciples as a group. Three times Peter denied that he knew Jesus. The third time he spoke vehemently and full of curses (Matthew 26:69-74).

After he was raised from the dead—This occurred after Jesus died and arose from the dead, but before He ascended to heaven.

Feed my lambs—Jesus owned no sheep, but He had cultivated the disciples, and there would be many new Christians to guide, protect, teach, and heal.

Peter was hurt because Jesus asked him the third time, "Do you love me?" He said, "Lord, you know all things; you know that I love you."

Jesus said, "Feed my sheep."

If you haven't read the notes in the shaded box, read them now. Take a minute to consider the following questions.

❶ After the passage is read, ask group members to read the explanations in the shaded box and jot down answers to the questions below. After a few minutes, have them choose one question and share their answer in a sentence or two. Anyone who wishes to pass may do so. Explain that this is not a time for discussion but for reporting responses to the questions.

Jesus

1. Which of these facts about Jesus catches your attention?

☐ He is a Savior who cooks.
☐ He is a Savior who offers help anonymously.
☐ Jesus isn't recognized one hundred yards away but is easily recognized for His miraculous works.
☐ He is a Savior who commissions an apostle in spite of his failures.
☐ Jesus, in His resurrected body, was capable of eating as well as walking through locked doors (Luke 24:40-43, John 20:26).
☐ Other:

2. This passage is full of images of Jesus as a nurturer and provider—helping them catch fish, handing them food He had cooked, telling them to feed His lambs. In what ways do you need to be nurtured or provided for?

Jesus' Questions for Peter

Here are some reasons offered for why Jesus asked Peter three times, "Do you love me?"

■ Asking "Do you love me?" three times paralleled Peter's three denials.
■ Jesus was trying to help Peter overcome his self-doubt about their relationship.
■ Peter had been the one to suggest going fishing (verse 3). Jesus probed to see if Peter loved Him more than the work of fishing (perhaps pointing to the nets and boat when He said, "Do you love me more than *these?*" emphasis added).
■ Jesus was trying to get Peter to examine his commitment to Him. (Peter once claimed, "I will lay down my life for you," (John 13:37-38) but then denied Jesus.)

3. If you had been Peter, what would have been most helpful to you about this interchange?

☐ Jesus singled me out for conversation.
☐ Jesus didn't seem to be mad.
☐ Jesus helped me look at my inner motives.
☐ Jesus accepted my less-than-perfect answers.
☐ Jesus gave me a commission to feed the sheep even though I had failed Him.
☐ Jesus kept challenging me to love Him, to do His work on earth.
☐ Jesus was still on this earth to talk to.

4. Who, if anyone, has welcomed you back into his or her life when you thought it could never happen?

5. By jumping out of the boat and swimming ashore, Peter was communicating something powerful to Jesus. By pulling Peter aside for conversation, Jesus was saying something to Peter. What were these two saying to each other?

6. If Jesus could pull you aside and say anything to you,

■ what would you like for it to be?
■ what do you think He would say (based on what God's been impressing on you lately)?

If any of the above questions are too difficult, hold them before God for a few minutes and then go on. Don't worry about getting an answer, but be open to what may come to you in the next few days.

Picturing the Passage   10-15 minutes
Before reading the passage again, consider these cues. Let them help you set the scene of how this event in Scripture might have occurred.

Cultural Cue: Fishing Habits
Night fishing was common, and it was probably a delightful experience to be out on the lake in the moonlight to fish all night and then come home tired. The disciples probably used grill nets, a long net fitted with floats that stayed in the water all night and were hauled in by boat the next day.[1]

Cultural Cue: The Breakfast Scene
When the disciples saw Jesus, they were about a hundred yards from the shore—the length of a football field (verse 8). As they scrambled to shore, they found the

tantalizing scene of their breakfast being cooked by a man who appeared utterly ordinary at first. The smell of grilled fish, the sight of a robed man squatting before a crackling fire—these were familiar. But looking closer, the disciples would have seen that the cook (Jesus) had a wounded side and hands that had been pierced with nails (John 20:27). Inside His sandals His feet bore huge wounds as He walked on a beach of pebbles and small shells.[2] How strange that must have been for the disciples—how difficult to keep from staring!

Setting Cue: Jesus and Peter Talk

When the conversation occurred, it was probably still morning and the disciples were resting from a full night of fishing and a big breakfast. Imagine the smell of the fire and burning coals.

Read the passage aloud this time and picture one of the scenes described in the cues above.

> ❶ Have group members read the cues silently. Then have a group member read the passage aloud while the others picture the passage.

Soaking In the Passage   5-15 minutes

Consider this all-important question whenever you read Scripture: How is my life touched by this passage today? Read the passage aloud again and ponder the following question for about five minutes: *What word, phrase, scene, or dramatic moment, sound, or smell emerges from the passage and stays with me?*

Here are some examples to consider:

☐ hearing John say, "It is the Lord," and Peter jumping into the water to swim ashore (verse 7)
☐ the smell of the coals Jesus prepared to provide breakfast for His disciples
☐ phrases (circle one): unable to haul the net in; Jesus came, took the bread and gave it to them; Do you love me? Feed my sheep.

After several minutes, write about the images or words that resonate with you from the passage.

Word or phrase:

Scene or moment: I hear . . . I see . . . I smell . . .

❶ Have a different group member read the passage aloud and then state the question printed in italics. Have group members sit quietly and then write the words, phrases, or images that come to mind. After a few minutes, ask group members to read what they've written. Anyone who wishes to pass may do so.

Pondering the Invitation   5-15 minutes
Perhaps God is offering you an invitation in this passage to do or be something different in your relationships. What might that be? Sit quietly for a few minutes, pondering this question: *What do I sense this passage calling me to do or be in my relationships with people?* If nothing comes, that's fine. Watch for insights in the next few days, but, for now, simply sit in the quiet and enjoy God's presence.

❶ Read the above instructions aloud, and after a few minutes repeat the question printed in italics. Ask group members to respond by saying, "I sense this passage calling me to. . . ." Then complete that statement with a short phrase. Anyone who wishes to pass may do so. Encourage members to listen respectfully and prayerfully to other group members.

Praying   5-10 minutes
Take a few minutes to respond to God about all of this. How do you feel about what you sensed (or didn't sense)? What do you most want to say to God?

❶ After allowing a few minutes for private prayer, ask group members to pray for the person on their left. Anyone wishing to pray silently may do so by saying, "I'm praying silently," and signifying when he or she is finished by saying "Amen."

Daily Lectio
If you wish, use the above format to meditate on God's Word between group meetings. You may wish to focus on today's passage every day this week (try using a different version of the Bible besides NIV), or you can use the following passages:

- Matthew 6:12-15 (forgiveness as Jesus taught in the Sermon on the Mount)
- Matthew 18:21-35 (parable of the unforgiving servant)
- Luke 23:32-43 (Jesus on the cross, forgiving the thief and His executioners)
- 2 Corinthians 2:5-11 (forgiving those who grieve us)
- Ephesians 4:29-32 (showing forgiveness and getting rid of bitterness)
- Colossians 3:12-14 (having compassion and kindness for others)

---

1. V. Gilbert Beers, *The Victor Journey Through the Bible* (Wheaton, Ill.: Victor Books, 1986), p. 341.
2. Beers, p. 340.

Developing a Generous Heart
Luke 6:37-45, Matthew 7:2

❶ After group members have greeted one another, ask them to close their eyes, relax their muscles, and breathe deeply. After they sit quietly for a few minutes, read the prayer in the "Warming Up" section. After a few more minutes, ask group members to share their thoughts about that prayer in a sentence or two. Anyone who wishes to pass may do so.

Warming Up   5-10 minutes
Center yourself by breathing in and out several times. Relax your neck and then take time to let your whole body relax. Offer each interruptive thought to God. Then consider this prayer for a few minutes:

> Give me the ability to see good things in unexpected places, and talents in unexpected people. And give me, O Lord, the grace to tell them so.[1]

If you wish, review the events of the past week, conversations with friends, and even what you've read in the newspaper. If nothing comes to you, that's fine. Try to enjoy God's presence without having to do anything.

Reading the Passage   15-20 minutes
You have probably heard the italicized phrases in the Scripture passage somewhere before. As you read, consider how the exact meaning of the words clarifies what it means to have a heart for other people. Read the explanations in the shaded box as you read the Scripture passage.

❶ Ask a group member to read the Scripture passage aloud. Suggest that other group members close their eyes as they listen.

Luke 6:37-45

TREATING PEOPLE WITH GENEROSITY

[37]"Do not *judge,* and you will not be judged. Do not condemn, and you will not be condemned. Forgive, and you will be forgiven. [For in the same way you judge others, you will be judged. Matthew 7:2] [38]Give, and it will be given to you. A good measure, *pressed down, shaken together and running over,* will be poured into your lap. For with the measure you use, it will be measured to you."

CHOOSING HEROES CAREFULLY

[39]He also told them this parable: *"Can a blind man lead* a blind man? Will they not both fall into a pit? [40]A student is not above his teacher, but everyone who is fully trained will be like his teacher.

LACK OF CREDENTIALS TO JUDGE

[41]"Why do you look at the *speck of sawdust in your brother's eye* and pay no attention to the plank in your own eye? [42]How can you say to your brother, 'Brother, let me take the speck out of your eye,' when you yourself fail to see the plank in your own eye? You *hypocrite*, first take the plank out of your eye, and then you will see clearly to remove the speck from your brother's eye.

INNER THOUGHTS COUNT

[43]No good tree bears bad fruit, nor does a bad tree bear good fruit. [44]Each tree is recognized by its own fruit. People do not pick figs from thornbushes, or grapes from briers. [45]The good man brings good things out of the good stored up in his heart, and the evil man brings evil

---

Judge—The original Greek word used here means to act as a judge of someone else. This involves passing judgment and condemnation, but it is not the same thing as discerning, examining, or questioning (these are appropriate things).

Pressed down, shaken together and running over—This was the method used to make sure buyers got a full basket or cup with no air pockets underneath.

Can a blind man lead—Blindness was mentioned thirty-four times in the gospels and was a common ailment because of poor sanitation and uncovered garbage, waste water, and toilets. Flies were abundant and spread diseases. Medicines were crude.

Speck of sawdust in your brother's eye—It's not that we are to ignore wrongdoing, but we should not judge motives.

Hypocrite—Not simply someone who says one thing and does another, but someone who doesn't even have a heart to do the right thing.

things out of the evil stored up in his heart. For out of the overflow of his heart his mouth speaks.

If you haven't read the notes in the shaded box, read them silently now. Take a minute to consider the following questions.

❶ After the passage is read, ask group members to read the explanations in the shaded box and jot down answers to the questions below. After a few minutes, have them choose one question and share their answer in a sentence or two. Anyone who wishes to pass may do so. Explain that this is not a time for discussion but for reporting responses to the questions.

Switching the Focus

1. Verse 38 presents an image of generosity in the form of a merchant making extra effort to be fair. As the merchant measures the grain, he or she makes sure buyers get the full amount they ordered, by pressing down the grain, shaking the cup, and filling it up until it runs over. Describe the kind of heart a merchant needs to have to measure in such a generous and fair way.

   What kind of expression can you imagine on such a merchant's face?

2. The first two paragraphs are about how we should treat other people. (The words *you* and *your* appear twenty-two times.) It's as if there's a mysterious linkage between how I treat others and how they treat me. This is called reciprocity—what goes around comes around. In our worst selves, however, we don't believe in reciprocity; we think we deserve special treatment. Even though I judge you harshly, I want you to judge me fairly and with understanding. In what area of life do you need to experiment with reciprocity?

   ☐ work
   ☐ family
   ☐ friendship
   ☐ neighborhood
   ☐ people in this study group

Judgment Nuances

3. Some might say these passages contradict each other. We're not to judge (Luke 6:37), but we are to evaluate leaders carefully enough to avoid following someone we believe is blind (Luke 6:39-40). How can we be discerning people without becoming judgmental? Here are some ideas to get you started:

- Discernment looks for facts, while judging looks to condemn.
- Judgment assumes authority over someone or superior wisdom, while discernment assumes equal authority.
- It boils down to an attitude of the heart.
- Other ideas:

Let's say a friend is struggling with an attraction to a married person of the opposite sex. What would be the difference between treating that person judgmentally or with discernment?

4. To get ready for a paraphrase exercise below, think of items that are different in size but the same in composition or function. Here are some examples:

LARGE ITEM	SMALL ITEM
glacier	ice chip
pizza restaurant oven	Bunsen burner
woolly mammoth	a strand of hair

Then read the verses below and insert the large item in the (1) blank and the small item in the (2) blank. Have fun with this. If you're not working in a group, read this aloud to yourself.

Luke 6:41-42 (paraphrased): Why do you look at the (2) _____ in your brother's eye and pay no attention to the (1)_____ in your own eye? How can you say to your brother, "Brother, let me take the (2) _____ out of your eye," when you yourself fail to see the (1) _____ in your own eye? You hypocrite, first take the (1) _____ out of your eye, and then you will see clearly to remove the (2) _____ from your brother's eye.

(If you like, stop here and doodle on page 166 a picture of yourself with a glacier or a restaurant oven in your eye.)

5. This passage helps us to see that our own faults handicap us from judging others fairly. What would a mere human need to be equipped to judge another? Add to this list:

- mind-reading skills
- thorough knowledge of the person's childhood and personal history
- extreme goodness to avoid showing partiality
- other:
- other:

6. Verse 45 highlights the idea that when we are inclining our heart to God, good behavior "accidentally" happens. When we're not, evil things "accidentally" happen. This explains why it's useless to try to change an attitude or outward behavior only. Actions and attitudes flow from the heart.

    Consider now a troublesome situation in which your actions seem to take over and you behave in ways that are inappropriate (for example, responding to a friend, family member, attractive members of the opposite sex). What is probably in your heart at that moment? What do you need to have already stored in your heart for you to behave appropriately?

Picturing the Passage   10-15 minutes
Before reading the passage again, consider these cues.

Character Cue: Jesus, as a Teacher
Even though you have heard these words many times, try to imagine how Jesus' first listeners felt. They probably laughed hard at Jesus' word picture of a plank sticking in someone's eye. Even worse, this visually handicapped person wanted to do minor eye surgery on someone else. Stop him, quickly!

How clever of Jesus to speak to us who are so deep in a moral wilderness, justifying ourselves for all kinds of harsh and judgmental behavior. Jesus enters with funny word pictures, showing us who we are. What a gentle way to jolt our conscience.

Setting Cue: The "Mount"
The accepted location of the Sermon on the Mount is a hilly region called the Horns of Hattin. This mountain has twin peaks with a craterlike formation in the middle.[2] If you were sitting in this remote setting with a huge crowd of people, it might be easier to hear Christ say things that hit home with you. Besides, people in Galilee weren't known for dotting each "i" and crossing each "t" in regard to the Law,[3] so they were probably eating up teaching that sounded unconventional to the Pharisees.

Read this passage aloud this time, then close your eyes and picture the images presented (the overflowing cup, a large item/small item of your own, a good tree bearing good fruit image that shows us we speak from the heart).

◐ Have group members read these cues and instructions silently. Then ask a group member to read the passage aloud while the others picture the passage.

Soaking In the Passage   5-15 minutes

Reflect for a moment on how your life is touched by this passage. Read the passage aloud again and ponder the following question for several minutes: *What word or phrase or image emerges from the passage and stays with me?* If you begin to latch on to something that is most evident, set it aside for a moment and see if anything else emerges.

If you wish, picture yourself as a merchant. Then ponder what the cup you offer others looks like. Is it the cup pressed down, shaken, and overflowing? If not, how does it look? Perhaps you're a stingy merchant or just a sloppy one, lacking discernment and wasting grain.

After several minutes, write the words or images that resonate with you from the passage.

Words or images:

◐ Have a different group member read the passage aloud and then state the question printed in italics. Have the group sit together quietly and then write the words or images that come to mind. After a few minutes, ask group members to read what they've written. Anyone who wishes to pass may do so.

Pondering the Invitation   5-15 minutes

Perhaps God is offering you an invitation in this passage to do or be something within the next few days. What might that be? Sit quietly for a few minutes, pondering this question: *What do I sense this passage calling me to do or be right now?* If nothing comes to mind, that's fine. Watch for insights in the next few days. But for now, simply sit in the quiet and enjoy God's presence.

◐ Read the instructions aloud and after a few minutes repeat the question printed in italics. Ask group members to respond by saying, "I sense this passage calling me to. . . ." Then complete that statement with a short phrase. Anyone who wishes to pass may do so.

Praying   5-10 minutes

Respond to God by telling Him how you feel about what you sensed or didn't sense during this meditation. If you need to present questions to God, do so.

❶ After allowing a few minutes for private prayer, ask group members to pray for the person on their left. Anyone wishing to pray silently may do so by saying, "I'm praying silently," and signifying when he or she is finished by saying "Amen."

Daily Lectio

If you wish, use the above format to meditate on God's Word between group meetings. You may wish to focus on today's passage every day this week, or you can use the following passages:

- Psalm 37:25-29 (the blessings that come to those with a generous heart)
- Psalm 112:5-10 (generosity makes us secure and joyful)
- Proverbs 11:24-27 (a generous and trusting person will be blessed)
- Romans 14:4-13 (let God be the judge)
- 1 Corinthians 4:1-5 (remain faithful to God and let Him judge)
- James 2:1-4 (avoid showing favoritism)

---

1. Anonymous, "Prayer of an Aging Woman," as quoted in Veronica Zundel, ed., *The Eerdmans Book of Famous Prayers* (Grand Rapids, Mich.: Eerdmans, 1983), p. 53.
2. V. Gilbert Beers, *The Victor Journey Through the Bible* (Wheaton, Ill.: Victor Books, 1986), p. 250.
3. Alfred Edersheim, *The Life and Times of Jesus the Messiah* (MA: Hendrickson Publishers, 1993), p. 156.

Partnering in Ministry
Philippians 2:19-23, 2 Timothy 1:3-7

---

❶ After group members have had a chance to greet each other, read the centering instructions in the "Warming Up" section. Then present to them the assignment to think of someone they know and let them reflect quietly for a few minutes. Repeat the statement and ask them to share their thoughts in a sentence or two. Anyone who wishes to pass may do so.

Warming Up   5-10 minutes

After you center yourself by breathing deeply and relaxing your muscles, use the following statement to help focus your thoughts for meditation on today's passages. If thoughts interrupt, set them aside, or write them down, if you need to. Think of someone you know, and consider what you'd like to say to them if you knew they would die tomorrow.

Close your eyes and take a few minutes to consider the people in your life and what they mean to you. If nothing comes to you after a few minutes, simply enjoy being quiet with God.

Reading the Passages   15-20 minutes

Read the following Scripture passages, noting the explanations in the shaded box.

❶ Ask a group member to read the Scripture passages aloud. Suggest that other group members close their eyes as they listen.

Philippians 2:19-23

PARTNERS (PAUL WRITING ABOUT TIMOTHY)

¹⁹I hope in the Lord Jesus to send Timothy to you soon, that I also may be cheered when I receive news about you. ²⁰I have no one else like

167

him, who takes a genuine interest in *your welfare.* [21]For everyone looks out for his own interests, not those of Jesus Christ. [22]But you know that Timothy has proved himself, because as a son with his father he has served with me in the work of the gospel. [23]I hope, therefore, to *send him* as soon as I see how things go with me.

---

2 Timothy 1:3-7

FRIENDS (PAUL WRITING TO TIMOTHY)

[3]I thank God, whom I serve, as my forefathers did, with a clear conscience, as night and day I constantly remember you in my prayers. [4]Recalling *your tears,* I long to see you, so that I may be filled with joy. [5]I have been reminded of your sincere faith, which first lived in *your grandmother Lois and in your mother Eunice* and, I am persuaded, now lives in you also. [6]For this reason I remind you to fan into flame the gift of God, which is in you through the laying on of my hands. [7]For God did not give us a spirit of timidity, but a spirit of power, of love and of self-discipline.

If you haven't read the notes in the shaded box, read them now. Take a minute to consider the following questions.

❶ After the passages are read, ask group members to read the explanations in the sidebar and jot down answers to the questions below. After a few minutes, have them choose one question and share their answer in a sentence or two. Anyone who wishes to pass may do so. Explain that this is not a time for discussion but for reporting responses to the questions.

Paul—An apostle-missionary who traveled extensively.

Timothy—A younger man, a missionary and pastor Paul had trained.

Your welfare—The growth of the Philippians.

Send him—Paul was in prison in Rome (or possibly Caesarea), and Timothy would take the news of Paul's trial or verdict to Philippi.

Your tears—Timothy had cried, probably when they parted company as Paul was arrested and taken to Rome.

Your grandmother Lois and in your mother Eunice—Although Timothy's father was Greek, his mother and grandmother were Jews who became Christians, possibly through Paul's ministry in their home city, Lystra (Acts 16:1).

Bonded in Purpose

1. Side-by-side relationships are ones in which people do not continually evaluate each other but move forward together toward a common purpose. Paul and Timothy had a relationship like that. They were both focused on the work of the gospel. As they traveled together, they must have laughed and cried many times, forging a strong relationship. When have you made a friend based on mutual purpose? If that friendship was different from other friendships, how was it different?

Others-Centered Love

2. Which of these others-centered characteristics of love have you experienced?

   ☐ willingness to part with someone dear for the sake of the gospel
   ☐ admiration for someone based on love for God, not his or her personal qualities
   ☐ not being written off, even though you have flaws

   Paul (an intense person, no doubt) didn't discount Timothy for his timidity. Paul valued Timothy because he, apparently unlike others who were only preoccupied with their own needs, cared about advancing the gospel.

3. Read the list of ways Paul encouraged Timothy (2 Timothy 1:3-7).

   ■ thanked God for his friend
   ■ prayed constantly for his friend
   ■ stated how he longed to see this friend
   ■ reviewed his friend's interesting spiritual history
   ■ encouraged his friend to use the gift God gave him
   ■ pointed his friend toward goals (power, love, and self-discipline)

   Which of these ways of encouragement would you most like to receive from a friend or relative?

   Which of these would you most like to give to a friend or relative?

Better Than Hallmark

4. Underline within these passages a "phrase of the week" or a "one-liner" that describes something about the kind of relationship you'd like to have with someone.

Picturing the Passages   10-15 minutes

Before reading the passages again, consider these cues.

Character Cue: Paul's Circumstances

The apostle Paul wrote Philippians from a house where he was kept under close guard at all times and was probably chained to a soldier. He wrote 2 Timothy from a cold prison cell with only his writing materials and a visitor or two. (He may not have had access to a toilet, and some prisoners were not given food. They depended on outsiders to bring the food.) He wrote to Timothy not long before he was executed by the emperor Nero, and he seemed to know this was his last chance to say to his friend and partner what he needed to say. He also passed on his responsibilities to this "dear son" (2 Timothy 1:2) and successor, who had spent twenty years as his associate.

Character Cue: Timothy, Reading Paul's Letter

Imagine Timothy reading Paul's letters. Timothy was free, and able to do the work he learned at Paul's side. Perhaps Timothy read these letters over and over, cherishing them and trying to remember the things he and Paul did together and what it had been like to be Paul's apprentice. Paul seems to have filled the father role in Timothy's life, yet Paul treated him respectfully as a close friend and partner.

Armed with these cues, read the passage aloud and then close your eyes and picture Paul and Timothy in each of their settings.

> ❶ Have group members read these cues silently. Then have a group member read the Scripture passages aloud while the others picture the passages.

Soaking In the Passage   5-15 minutes

Reflect on how these Scripture passages touch your life today. Read the passages aloud again and ponder the following question for several minutes: *What word, phrase, scene, or image emerges from the passages and stays with me?* If you begin to latch on to something that is most evident, set it aside for a minute and wait to see if anything else emerges.

After several minutes, record the images or words that resonate with you from the passages.

Word or phrase:

Scene or image:

I hear . . . I see . . .

❶ Have a different group member read the passages aloud and then state the question printed in italics. Have the group sit quietly together and then write the words or images that come to mind. After a few minutes, ask group members to read what they've written. Anyone who wishes to pass may do so.

Pondering the Invitation   5-15 minutes

Perhaps God is offering you an invitation in these passages to do or be something within the next few days. What might that be? Sit quietly for a few minutes, pondering this question: *What do I sense these passages calling me to do or be right now?* In what relationship is God nudging me to move out and take a risk? If nothing comes to mind, that's fine. Simply sit in the quiet and enjoy God's presence.

❶ Read the above instructions aloud and after a few minutes repeat the question printed in italics. Ask group members to respond by saying, "I sense these passages calling me to. . . ." Then complete that statement with a short phrase. Anyone who wishes to pass may do so.

Praying   5-10 minutes

Take a few minutes to respond to God about all of this. How do you feel about what you sensed (or didn't sense)? What is it you most want to say to God at this time?

❶ After allowing a few minutes for private prayer, ask group members to pray for the person on their left. Anyone wishing to pray silently may do so by saying, "I'm praying silently," then signifying when he or she is finished by saying "Amen."

Daily Lectio

If you wish, use the above format to meditate on God's Word between group meetings. You may wish to focus on today's passages every day this week, or you can use the following passages:

- Ephesians 1:15-21 (a prayer for others)
- Ephesians 3:14-21 (a prayer for others)

- Philippians 1:3-8 (appreciation of others)
- Philippians 1:9-11 (a prayer for others)
- Colossians 1:9-12 (a prayer for others)
- 1 Thessalonians 2:6-12 (nurturing relationships with fellow workers)

Looking Beyond Ourselves
Philippians 2:1-4,14-16

> ❶ After group members have had a chance to greet each other, read the centering instructions in the "Warming Up" section. Then present the quiet question and let them reflect on it for a few minutes. Repeat the question and ask them to share their thoughts in a sentence or two. Anyone who wishes to pass may do so.

Warming Up   5-10 minutes

Center yourself by breathing in and out several times. Relax your neck and then take time to relax other muscles. Offer your distracting thoughts to God, one by one. Ask yourself the following quiet question to help focus on today's passage: What has God been saying to me recently about my behavior in relationships?

Close your eyes and take a few minutes to quietly consider your interaction with friends, coworkers, and family members to see if anything comes to you. If nothing comes to mind, simply enjoy keeping company with God.

Reading the Passage   15-20 minutes

Read the Scripture passage printed below, noting the explanations in the shaded box.

> ❶ Ask a group member to read the Scripture passage aloud. Suggest that other group members close their eyes as they listen.

Philippians 2:1-4,14-16

GIVING AS WE'RE GIVEN TO

¹If you have any encouragement from being united with Christ, if any comfort from his love, if any fellowship with the Spirit, if any tenderness

and compassion, ²then make my joy complete by being like-minded, having the same love, being one in spirit and purpose.

LOOKING OUTSIDE OURSELVES

³Do nothing out of selfish ambition or *vain* conceit, but in *humility* consider others better than yourselves. ⁴Each of you should look not only to your own interests, but also to the interests of others.

TRUSTING GOD THROUGHOUT

¹⁴Do everything without complaining or arguing, ¹⁵so that you may become *blameless* and *pure,* children of God without fault in a crooked and depraved generation, in which you shine like stars in the universe ¹⁶as you hold out the word of life — in order that I may *boast* on the day of Christ that I did not run or labor for nothing.

If you haven't read the notes in the shaded box, read them now. Take a minute to consider the following questions.

❶ After the passage is read, ask group members to read the explanations in the shaded box and then jot down answers to the questions below. After a few minutes, have them choose one question and share their answer in a sentence or two. Anyone who wishes to pass may do so. Explain that this is not a time for discussion but for reporting responses to the questions.

Union with God

1. Paul, the apostle who wrote this passage, used a lot of "if . . . then" clauses. Simplifying Paul's complicated "if . . . then" clauses in verses 1-2 might result in this paraphrase: "If you're experiencing union with God, then do what it takes to unite yourself with others." Paul expanded on the idea of experiencing union with God in these ways:

   ■ being encouraged by this union
   ■ finding comfort in God's love
   ■ fellowshipping with the Spirit
   ■ experiencing the tenderness and compassion of God

Vain—Egotistical or empty, self-glorifying; pushing your way to the front.[1]

Humility—Not pushing yourself ahead.

Blameless—A person who can't be blamed for things; uncorrupted.

Pure—Harmless, sincere, used to describe wine unmixed with water, or unalloyed metal; hence without mixed motives; a breath of fresh air in a polluted society.[2]

Boast—Brag, but in the sense of rejoicing; Paul would be proud of the Philippians.

Reread these phrases and look at them for a minute or two. Then check the ones you've experienced within the last few months.

If you have other thoughts about any of the phrases, write a few sentences about those thoughts. (For example, you may be thinking, *I have no idea what any of those phrases really mean! Speak to me, God.*)

Unity with Each Other

2. Paul expanded on the idea of uniting ourselves with others in the following ways:

☐ loyalty toward each other even when we don't agree
☐ loving each other with the self-sacrificing love of Christ
☐ harmony of feeling
☐ having common purposes and goals[3]

When have you experienced these movements of God?

Again, if you need to ponder this or write about it, do so at the end of the session. (For example, you may be thinking, *Is it possible to feel that way about anyone who isn't already a close friend?*)

3. The phrase, "consider others better than yourselves," is not suggesting that we have low self-worth; it is a teaching about not being self-absorbed. It urges us to ask, *Do I give most of my thoughts and time to meeting my own needs? Is everything I do and think about me?* It's human nature to be self-obsessed, but God urges us to be self-forgetful.

Consider what you might say to God, or ask Him, when you find yourself absorbed in selfish ambition, personal prestige, trying to impress people, or popularity.

■ What does this other person need?
■ Help me to see that everything isn't about me.
■ Your idea:

■ Your idea:

Trusting God Throughout

4. "Do everything without complaining or arguing" (verse 14) doesn't mean that we shouldn't ask questions or make suggestions, but that we need to look at our hearts. Ask yourself, *Do I have a reconciler's heart or a complainer's heart?* Answer the following question about yourself.

Before I complain or disagree with someone, I . . .

☐ try to see what's going on inside the person involved
☐ pray for the person involved
☐ try to get to know the person involved
☐ ask myself if I have any reason to hold a grudge against the person or cause
☐ your idea:

Picturing the Passage   10-15 minutes
Before reading the passage aloud this time, consider these cues.

Character Cue: The Philippian Church
The readers of Paul's letter were a varied group (Acts 16:12-40):

- a prison jailer (middle-class civil servant) who almost killed himself when he thought Paul had escaped. Paul stopped him, and he and his family were baptized;
- a rich fabric merchandiser, Lydia, with whom Paul and Silas stayed;
- a slave girl fortuneteller, who had been demon-possessed.

The Philippian church may have included or been visited by:

- the slave girl's owners who had Paul and Silas arrested;
- members of the crowd who attacked Paul and Silas;
- those who beat Paul and Silas;
- town officers who ordered them to be stripped and beaten, later found out they were Roman citizens, and tried to appease them.

Put yourself in the place of a reader. Who would have been the most difficult for you to "consider better than yourself"? The slave girl? Those who beat Paul and Silas? The town officers who ordered the beating?

Setting Cue: The City, Philippi
Philippi was a place where things happened. It was a Roman colony and the leading city of the district of Macedonia. Named for Philip of Macedon (master of Greece and father of Alexander the Great), Philippi focused on trade and getting ahead. Paul's words about humility and unity must have been radical!

When Paul and Silas first went to Macedonia, they preached outside the city gate by the river. The church may have continued to meet there beyond the watchful eyes of city officials.

Now read the Scripture passage aloud this time and then close your eyes, picturing this letter being read to the Philippian church as they sit by the river with its outdoor sounds and scents.

❶ Have group members read these cues silently. Then ask a group member to read the passage aloud while the others picture the passage.

Soaking In the Passage   5-15 minutes

Consider how your life is a mirror of this passage, or how you think God wants it to be. Read the passage aloud once more and ponder the following question for several minutes: *What word, phrase, scene, sound, or smell emerges from the passage and stays with me?* If you latch on to something quickly, set it aside for a moment and see what else emerges.

After several minutes, record the words or images that resonate with you from the passage.

Word or phrase:

Scene or image: I hear . . . I see . . .

❶ Have a different group member read the passage aloud and then state the question printed in italics. Have the group sit quietly for a while and then record the words or images that come to mind. After a few minutes, ask group members to read what they've written. Anyone who wishes to pass may do so.

Pondering the Invitation   5-15 minutes

Perhaps God is inviting you to walk with Him more deeply in some way. Sit quietly for a few minutes, pondering this question: *What do I need to know from this passage?* If nothing comes to mind, that's fine. Watch for insights in the next few days, but for now, simply sit in the quiet and enjoy God's presence.

❶ Read the instructions aloud, and after a few minutes, repeat the question printed in italics. Ask group members to respond by saying, "I sense this passage calling me to. . . ." Then complete that statement with a short phrase. Anyone who wishes to pass may do so.

Praying   5-10 minutes

Respond to God by telling Him how you feel about what you sensed (or didn't sense) during this meditation. What do you need to say to God, if anything, at this time? If you need to present questions to God, do so.

❶ After allowing a few minutes for private prayer, ask group members to pray for the person on their left. Anyone wishing to pray silently may do so by saying, "I'm praying silently," then signifying when he or she is finished by saying "Amen."

Daily Lectio

If you wish, use the above format to meditate on God's Word between group meetings. You may wish to focus on today's passage every day this week, or you can use the following passages:

- Proverbs 16:28 (the effects of dissension and gossip)
- Romans 14:15-19 (making efforts for peace)
- Philippians 2:5-13 (Christ humbling Himself as a servant)
- Colossians 3:12-14 (the forgiving character of a Christian)
- Titus 3:1-5 (being peaceable and considerate)
- James 3:13-18 (wisdom versus selfish ambition)

---

1. Eugene Peterson, *The Message* (Colorado Springs, Colo.: NavPress, 1993), p. 414.
2. Peterson, p. 415.
3. Based on meaning of Greek words and phrases as explained in Gerald F. Hawthorne, *World Biblical Commentary: Philippians* (Waco, Tex.: Word, 1983), p. 68.

Connecting with Others as Life Falls Apart

Ruth 1:8,13-18; 2:11,19-20; 3:1; 4:13-16

❶ After group members have had a chance to greet each other, read the centering instructions in the "Warming Up" section. Then present the quiet question and let them reflect quietly for a few minutes. Repeat the question and ask them to share their thoughts in a sentence or two. Anyone who wishes to pass may do so.

Warming Up   5-10 minutes

Center yourself by breathing in and out several times. Relax your neck and then relax other muscles. If thoughts interrupt, set them aside or write them down. Ask yourself the following question to help focus your thoughts for meditation on today's passage: What does God want me to be in my relationships with others? Give your answer in the form of an object—a household gadget, a yard or car tool, or some other object. Close your eyes and take a few minutes to see yourself in relationship with others.

Reading the Passage   15-20 minutes

If you've heard the story of Ruth and Naomi before, set aside what you know and view them for their strength of character. Read the Scripture passage printed below, noting the explanations in the shaded box.

❶ Ask a group member to read the Scripture passage aloud. Suggest that other group members close their eyes as they listen.

Ruth 1:8,13-18; 2:11,19-20; 3:1; 4:13-16

TRAGEDY STRIKES

1:8Then *Naomi* said to her two daughters-in-law, "Go back, each of you, to your mother's home. May the LORD show kindness to you, as you have shown to your dead and to me. . . . 13It is more bitter for me than for you, because the LORD's hand has gone out against me."

14Then Orpah kissed her mother-in-law good-by, but Ruth clung to her.

15"Look," said Naomi, "your sister-in-law is going back to her people and her gods. Go back with her."

16But Ruth replied, "Don't urge me to leave you or to turn back from you. Where you go I will go, and where you stay I will stay. Your people will be my people and your God my God. 17Where you die I will die, and there I will be buried. May the LORD deal with me, be it ever so severely, if anything but death separates you and me." 18When Naomi realized that Ruth was determined to go with her, she stopped urging her.

RETURN TO ISRAEL

2:11Boaz replied, "I've been told all about what you [Ruth] have done for your mother-in-law since the death of your husband—how you left your father and mother and your homeland and came to live with a people you did not know before.

2:19Her mother-in-law asked her, "Where did you *glean* today? Where did you work? Blessed be the man who *took notice of you*!"

Then Ruth told her mother-in-law about the one at whose place she had been working. "The name of the man I worked with today is Boaz," she said. . . . 20[Naomi] added, "That man is our close relative; he is one of our *kinsman-redeemers*."

Naomi—This Israelite woman and her husband had gone to live in Moab, a foreign country. After her sons married Moabite women, her husband and two sons died. A widow faced with starvation, she decided to try to return to Israel.

Glean—A law in Israel (Leviticus 19:9, 23:22) that allowed the poor to follow the reapers and gather the grain left behind. Gathering these stalks was not easy.

Took notice of you—Naomi noticed that the reapers had left quite a bit behind, and she assumed they did it on purpose to help Ruth. This was true (2:15-16).

Kinsman-redeemers—close relatives who had the right to buy property of the deceased and to marry the wife of the deceased.

Boaz took Ruth and she became his wife—Boaz was attracted to Ruth because of her kindness to Naomi. Then through Naomi's wise counsel, Ruth gained his attention even further.

SECURITY AND FAMILY RESTORED

[3:1]One day Naomi her mother-in-law said to her, "My daughter, should I not try to find a home for you, where you will be well provided for?" [4:13]So *Boaz took Ruth and she became his wife*. Then he went to her, and the Lord enabled her to conceive, and she gave birth to a son. [14]The women said to Naomi: "Praise be to the LORD, who this day has not left you without a kinsman-redeemer. . . .[15]For your daughter-in-law, who loves you and who is better to you than seven sons, has given him birth."

[16]Then Naomi took the child, laid him in her lap and cared for him.

If you haven't read the notes in the shaded box, read them now. Take a minute to consider the following questions.

> ❶ After the passage is read, ask group members to read the explanations in the shaded box and then jot down answers to the questions below. After a few minutes, have them choose one question and share their answer in a sentence or two. Anyone who wishes to pass may do so. Explain that this is not a time for discussion but for reporting responses to the questions.

Ruth and Naomi's Relationship

1. Check the qualities listed below that you think describe Naomi.

   ☐ strong-minded
   ☐ listens to others
   ☐ confident
   ☐ bold
   ☐ controlling
   ☐ assertive
   ☐ easily swayed

   In what ways was Naomi good to Ruth?

2. Check the qualities listed below that you think describe Ruth.

   ☐ strong-minded
   ☐ listens to others
   ☐ confident
   ☐ bold
   ☐ controlling
   ☐ assertive
   ☐ easily swayed

In what ways was Ruth good to Naomi?

3. These two women traveled together, lived together, probably starved together a few nights. What would it have taken for these two women to have gotten along?

4. Ruth seems to have been obeying the italicized phrase in these verses: "Two are better than one, because they have a good return for their work: *If one falls down, his friend can help him up.* But pity the man who falls and has no one to help him up!" (Ecclesiastes 4:9-10, emphasis added). In turn, Naomi tried to help Ruth by coaching her in marriage matters. Can you think of a time when you "helped someone up" and they also helped you? If so, ponder the value of the help you gave.

Picturing the Passage   10-15 minutes
Before reading the passage again, consider these cues.

Character Cue: Naomi's Good Will
This woman invalidated the myth that all mothers-in-law are controlling. Not only did Naomi try to keep her daughters-in-law from going with her (for their own good), but when Ruth insisted, she gave in. She also didn't try to keep Ruth to herself but began thinking about how Ruth could link up with her family's kinsman-redeemer.

Character Cue: Ruth's Motives
Going with Naomi on that journey was not a clever choice, and we can only guess why Ruth did it. Perhaps she wanted to attach herself to God and to Naomi's people, Israel. She implied that she believed in Jehovah God: "May the LORD deal with me, be it ever so severely, if anything but death separates you and me."

Cultural Cue: Plight of Widows
The passage opens with one of the most destitute situations in Scripture—three widows without sons. In those times, widows got absolutely nothing. A deceased

man's property went to the man who owned the family birthright. If no one helped the widow, she spent the rest of her life in extreme poverty. Because a widow had no male to protect her, people often took advantage of her. Israelite law stated that the son should care for a widow, but these three women had no sons! In that case, they returned to their parents (as Orpah did) to live a life of near-servant status. Ruth stayed with Naomi, but neither of them had anything.

Contrast this with the end of the account. Naomi and Ruth not only survived, but Ruth's remarriage meant they would also be cared for and have the thing that gave an Israelite woman the biggest boost in her self-worth: a son.

Cultural Cue: The "Alien" or "Stranger"

Scripture required godly people then, as now, to care for certain groups of people who are likely to be forgotten and abused. Widows are one of those groups, as are "alien[s]" (NIV) or "stranger[s]" (KJV). In those days, there were foreigners and immigrants who came to Israel. A certain class of "strangers" (of which Ruth seems to have been a part) put themselves under the protection of Israel's God. They often submitted to many requirements of the law of Israel and also received some of the privileges.[1] But aliens were not always treated well, as evidenced by the need to command Jews not to oppress the alien (Zechariah 7:10).

So imagine Ruth, a young foreign woman, gleaning in the fields. It was providential that Boaz commanded his men not to harm her (Ruth 2:9). She must have been a brave woman to have come to a foreign country destitute but eager to make a way for Naomi and herself.

Setting Cue: Their Journey

Naomi and Ruth traveled together from the land of Moab to the town of Bethlehem in southern Israel. It's difficult to imagine how these two made the journey. They had to walk through the hilly country of Moab around the Dead Sea—about seventy miles along the trade routes. How did they cross the Jordan River, one wonders? People probably took them in at night and may have given them food for the next day. Daytime temperatures in Palestine can be in excess of 100 degrees, although in the hill country the evening temperature can fall sharply, and the nights can be chilly.[2]

Armed with the above cues, read the passage aloud and then close your eyes, picturing the events as if they were a movie playing in your mind. Work through each scene, imagining the sights, sounds, and smells. Here are some images to get you started:

- tragedy strikes
- the trip home to Israel
- gleaning in the fields and meeting Boaz
- forming a new family with Boaz

❶ Have group members read the cues silently. Then have a group member read the passage aloud while the others picture the events.

Soaking In the Passage   5-15 minutes

Reflect on how this Scripture passage touches your life today. Read the passage aloud again and ponder the following question for several minutes: *What word or phrase, scene or image emerges from the passage and stays with me?* After several minutes, write the word, phrase, images, or scenes that resonate within you from the passage.

Word or phrase:

Scene or image: I hear . . . I see . . .

> ❶ Ask a different group member to read the passage aloud and then state the question printed in italics. Have the group sit quietly for a while and then write down the words or images that come to mind. After a few minutes, ask group members to read what they've written. Anyone who wishes to pass may do so.

Pondering the Invitation   5-15 minutes

Perhaps God is offering you an invitation in this passage to do or be something within the next few days. What might that be? Sit in silence for a few minutes, pondering this question: *What do I sense this passage calling me to do or be right now?* Be open to the quiet, but don't feel pressured to come up with something.

> ❶ Read the above instructions aloud. After a few minutes, repeat the question printed in italics. Ask group members to respond by saying, "I sense this passage calling me to. . . ." Then complete that statement with a short phrase. Anyone who wishes to pass may do so.

Praying   5-10 minutes

Take a few minutes to respond to God about this meditation. How do you feel about what you sensed (or didn't sense)? What is it you most want to say to God at this time?

> ❶ After allowing a few minutes for private prayer, ask group members to pray for the person on their left. Anyone wishing to pray silently may do so by saying, "I'm praying silently," and signifying when he or she is finished by saying "Amen."

Daily Lectio

If you wish, use the above format to meditate on God's Word between group meetings. You may wish to focus on today's passage every day this week, or you can use the following passages:

- Psalm 68:4-10 (God provides family for widows)
- Psalm 146:1-10 (God provides for widows and aliens)
- Proverbs 17:17 (friends through adversity)
- Ecclesiastes 4:9-12 (why two are better than one)
- Galatians 6:9-10 (caring for others, especially fellow believers)
- 1 Timothy 5:4-8 (caring for family members)

---

1. Merrill C. Tenney, *The Zondervan Pictorial Bible Dictionary* (Grand Rapids, Mich.: Zondervan, 1967), p. 812.
2. J. A. Thompson, *Handbook of Life in Bible Times* (Downers Grove, Ill.: InterVarsity Press, 1986), p. 21.

PART SIX

MOVING BEYOND MEDIOCRITY

When You Want to Discern
God's Purpose for Your Life

How God Changes People
through Meditation

As we come to know and rely on God and surrender more of ourselves to Him, He transforms us. Our character changes, and we become different people. Our hearts of stone become hearts of flesh.

One way to cooperate with His plan of transformation—"be transformed by the renewing of your mind" (Romans 12:2)—is to encounter God through the living, productive, penetrating Word of God. That encounter massages the mind, heart, and even the imagination so that we taste and see that the Lord is good (Psalm 34:8). This process directly affects our behavior: "Do not let this Book of the Law depart from your mouth; meditate on it day and night, *so that you may be careful to do everything written in it*" (Joshua 1:8, emphasis added). How does that happen?

Transformation means looking at the sealed, stale rooms of ourselves and offering all we find to God for forgiveness, acceptance, and healing. It doesn't happen quickly. All along the way there are flashes of insight, moments of exquisite beauty, experiences of reconciliation. We are clay, responding to the hands of the Potter and His gradual shaping. Participating fully in *lectio* is a sign that we are conscious and cooperative clay. Transformation occurs slowly—little by little—when we see our true self and let go of it a little more.

Slowly you'll notice how the detachment learned in meditation carries over into all of life. In meditation, we learn to turn the thought-tapes in our heads into prayer, or we learn to set negative thoughts aside and give them less control over our actions. For instance, we can detach a little easier when we're getting on the freeway and another driver is rude to us. We can say to ourselves, *This isn't a crisis; I have too much good going on with God to be bothered by this.*

Handling Fearful, Fussy People
Exodus 14: 10-16,19-22

❶ After group members have had a chance to greet each other, read the centering instructions in the "Warming Up" section (see bullets). Then present the quiet questions and let them reflect for a few minutes. Repeat the questions and ask them to share their thoughts in a sentence or two. Anyone who wishes to pass may do so. After group members share, thank them and comment that it's helpful to hear the variety of ways God speaks to people.

Warming Up   5-10 minutes

Before answering the questions below, sit quietly for about two minutes. To help center yourself, try the following:

- Breathe in and out deeply five or six times. Relax your neck and move it around. Then let your arms go limp and relax your legs and ankles. Relax each part from the inside out.
- Use the "palms down, palms up" method to turn your distractions over to God. Rest your hands in your lap, placing palms down whenever you think of concerns you need to turn over to God. Turn your palms up as a symbol of your desire to receive from the Lord and set aside distractions.

Ask yourself the following quiet questions to help focus your thoughts for meditation on today's passage: When have I been involved in a project much bigger than myself? How did I feel about it? Close your eyes and take a few minutes to quietly consider the events of your life and see if anything comes to you.

Reading the Passage   15-20 minutes

Read silently the following passage, noting the explanations in the shaded box.

❶ To set the scene for this passage, read aloud the note "As Pharaoh approached" in the shaded box on page 190. Then ask a group member to read the Scripture passage aloud. Suggest that other group members close their eyes as they listen.

Exodus 14:10-16,19-22

ISRAEL COMPLAINS

[10]*As Pharaoh approached,* the Israelites looked up, and there were the Egyptians, marching after them. They were *terrified* and cried out to the LORD. [11]They said to Moses, "Was it because there were no graves in Egypt that you brought us to the desert to die? What have you done to us by bringing us out of Egypt? [12]Didn't we say to you in Egypt, 'Leave us alone; let us serve the Egyptians'? It would have been better for us to serve the Egyptians than to die in the desert!"

MOSES TALKS BACK TO THEIR TERROR

[13]Moses answered the people, "Do not be afraid. Stand firm and you will see the deliverance the Lord will bring you today. The Egyptians you see today you will never see again. [14]The LORD will fight for you; you need only to be still."

[15]Then the LORD said to Moses, "Why are you crying out to me? Tell the Israelites to move on. [16]Raise your staff and stretch out your hand over *the sea* to divide the water so that the Israelites can go through the sea on dry ground.

THE ANGEL KEEPS WATCH

[19]Then the angel of God, who had been traveling in front of Israel's army, withdrew and went behind them. The pillar of cloud also moved from in front and stood behind them, [20]coming between the armies of Egypt and Israel. Throughout the night the cloud brought darkness to the one side and light to the other side; so neither went near the other all night long.

GOD MIRACULOUSLY DELIVERS ISRAEL

[21]Then Moses stretched out his hand over the sea, and all that night the Lord drove the sea back with a strong east wind and turned it into dry land. The waters were divided, [22]and the Israelites went through the sea on dry ground, with a wall of water on their right and on their left.

As Pharaoh approached—At this point, Moses and Israel have watched God bring the ten plagues on Egypt to force the Pharaoh to let Israel go. They have left Egypt for freedom, but here come the Egyptians chasing them.

Terrified—Their terror is evidenced by their appalling remarks as they overlooked the cruel way they were treated in Egypt (verses 11-12).

The sea—Most scholars agree that the Hebrew words would be better rendered, "reed sea" or "marsh sea." This then refers to a body of water north of the Red Sea and not the Red Sea itself.

If you haven't read the notes in the shaded box, read them silently now. Take a minute to consider the following questions.

❶ After the passage is read, ask group members to read silently the explanations in the shaded box and then jot down answers to the questions below. After a few minutes, have them choose one question and share their answer in a sentence or two. Anyone who wishes to pass may do so. Explain that this is not a time for discussion but for reporting responses to the questions.

When Purposes Are Nearly Defeated

1. When we venture out for God into the purposes we believe He has instilled in us, we often go through this scenario:

- Terror and complaints: Why did I get into this? What made me think I could do this? Why did God let me do this? I want out!
- We talk back to our terror: God got us into this—God will get us out. Hold on!
- God keeps watch: There's silence or a standstill, and the suspense is staggering.
- God miraculously delivers: Our dream finally comes true.

Inside each of the three shaded headings in the chart below, write a purpose, cause, job, or calling in which you are now involved—planning an event, raising a child, staying married, volunteering in a certain position, and so on.

Then below each shaded space, place a check mark in one of the rows to indicate where you are in that calling: terrified/complaining? talking back to the terror? keeping watch with God? finding a miraculous deliverance? Or, write in your own stage and put a check mark beside that.

	Purpose 1:	Purpose 2:	Purpose 3:
Terror & complaints			
Talking back to terror			
God keeps watch			
Miraculous deliverance			
Some other stage: (write it in)			

2. *Terror and complaints:* Terror robbed the Israelites of their clear thinking. Look how they behaved:

WHAT THE ISRAELITES SAID	HOW THEY ERRED
"Was it because there were no graves in Egypt that you brought us to the desert to die?" verse 11	They accused Moses (whom God chose to help them) of sabotaging their chance for a decent burial.
"Didn't we say to you in Egypt, 'Leave us alone; let us serve the Egyptians'? It would have been better for us to serve the Egyptians than to die in the desert!" verse 12	They distorted their memories of their terrible life in slavery.

When have you, in terror, done one of the following?

- lashed out at the person who helped you the most
- acted as if the alternative wasn't so bad after all
- been the leader and received all this terror and complaining

3. *Talking back to terror:* Moses encouraged the Israelites by doing the first two things in the list below. Which, if any, of the things on this list have you done or said to encourage yourself or others?

☐ Pointed them to a certain future (you will see the deliverance, verse 13)
☐ Urged them to have confidence in God (God will fight for you, verse 14)
☐ Remembered God's past track record of rescue
☐ Listed reasons why what you or another is doing is important within God's kingdom
☐ Other:

4. *God keeps watch:* How do you behave during lulls in the storm? (Check as many as you like.)

☐ I obsess over solutions, as if my obsessing will solve something.
☐ I sometimes manage to pray about the situation.
☐ I try to forget about it so I won't be bothered.
☐ Other:

5. *Miraculous deliverance:* How do you respond when tension is released and the problem is solved?

☐ I'm so relieved that I forget to thank God.
☐ I call people and tell them about it.
☐ I record it in my journal.
☐ I have a party with my friends and try not to gloat over my enemies.
☐ Other:

If any of the above questions are too difficult, hold them before God for a few minutes and then go on. Don't worry about getting an answer, but be open to what may come to you in the next few days.

Picturing the Passage   10–15 minutes
Before reading the passage again, consider these cues. Use them to set the scene for this scriptural event.

Geographical Cue: Egypt Versus the Desert
The Israelites were treated cruelly in Egypt, but Egypt had a lot going for it—fertile land, the water of the Nile River, and a surplus of food and bread (Exodus 16:3). The Israelites left behind the lush Nile Delta region and headed for another beautiful area—Canaan. But in between lay a desert with little water and almost no trees. In the desert they faced nomadic tribes, outlaws, lack of water, sparse vegetation, serpents, and wild animals.[1]

Geographical Cue: The Sea
Many scholars believe that the Red Sea, or "reed sea," was Lake Timsah. The Scripture itself provides clues for the imagination: it was deep enough to create walls of water on the side, and when the walls were released, there was enough water to drown the pursuing Egyptians—six hundred of the best chariots, along with all the other chariots of Egypt (Exodus 14:7, 22, 28-30).
Read the scenes below and then choose one of them to picture. As you do so, put yourself in the place of Moses or a typical Israelite:

- *Israel complains:* The Israelites were trapped between the sea and the mountains with the Egyptians approaching from behind. The Egyptian Pharaoh was coming with his six hundred chariots, as well as other chariots and horses (14:7).
- *Moses talks back to their terror:* God had already warned Moses that they would be hemmed in, that the Egyptians would pursue them, and that he, God, would "gain glory" (14:1-4). What a challenge for Moses to communicate this to Israel.
- *God keeps watch:* At this point, Moses had already stretched out his hand

over the sea and God had told him the Israelites would walk through it on dry ground (14:15-18). It must have been a suspenseful night with the angel hovering. Imagine the angel and the cloud as they moved from in front of Israel to behind Israel and in front of the Egyptians. We don't know if the angel was visible, but the light shone on Israel and the Egyptians waited in the darkness.

■ *God miraculously delivers Israel:* Given a way out through the water, the complaining Israelites picked up their gear and walked over the dry ground. Imagine the wall of water on the right and left. We don't know if they could see the underwater creatures or how the wall looked.

Read the Scripture passage aloud and use the above material to imagine how this scriptural event might have occurred.

❶ Have group members read these cues and scene descriptions silently. Then ask a group member to read the passage aloud while the others picture the passage.

Soaking In the Passage   5-15 minutes

Consider now this all-important question to address whenever you read Scripture: How is my life touched by this passage today? Read the passage aloud again and ponder the following question for about five minutes: *What scene or dramatic moment emerges from the passage and stays with me?* For example, you might want to picture:

☐ the Egyptians approaching in their six hundred-plus chariots
☐ Moses raising his staff and stretching his hand over the sea
☐ the angel of God moving to come between the Israelites and the Egyptians
☐ phrases (circle one): do not be afraid; stand firm; be still

After several minutes, write below the scenes or images that resonate with you from the passage.

I hear . . . I see . . .

❶ Have a different group member read the passage aloud and then state the question printed in italics. Ask members to write the word or image from the passage that stays in their minds. After the group reflects quietly for a few minutes, ask group members to read what they've written.

Pondering the Invitation

Perhaps God is offering you an invitation in this passage to do or be something within the next few days. What might that be? Reflect quietly for at a few minutes, pondering this question: *What do I need to know for my life right now?* If nothing comes to mind, that's fine. Watch for insights in the next few days, but for now, simply sit in the quiet and enjoy God's presence.

> ❶ Read the above instructions aloud. After a few minutes, repeat the question printed in italics. Ask group members to respond by saying, "I sense this passage calling me to know. . . ." Then complete that statement with a short phrase. Anyone who wishes to pass may do so.

Praying

Take a few minutes to respond to God about this meditation. How do you feel about what you sensed (or didn't sense)? What is it you most want to say to God at this time?

> ❶ After allowing a few minutes for private prayer, ask group members to pray for the person on their left. Anyone wishing to pray silently may do so by saying, "I'm praying silently," then signifying when he or she is finished by saying "Amen."

Daily Lectio

If you wish, use the above format to meditate on God's Word between group meetings. You may wish to focus on today's passage every day this week (try using a version of the Bible different from NIV), or you can use the following passages:

- Exodus 3:1-12 (God calls Moses from the burning bush)
- Exodus 15:1-18 (song of victory sung by Moses and the Israelites)
- Exodus 15:20-21 (Miriam's song of victory)
- Psalm 105:1-10 (remembering God's miracles)
- Isaiah 49:6-12 (Israel a light to the Gentiles)
- Jeremiah 29:11-13 (God gave purpose to Israel)

---

1. V. Gilbert Beers, *The Victor Journey Through the Bible* (Wheaton, Ill.: Victor Books, 1986), pp. 64-65.

God Gives Me Purpose in Life
Matthew 7:7-11

---

❶ After group members have had a chance to greet each other, read the centering instructions in the "Warming Up" section. Then present the quiet question and let them reflect for a few minutes. Repeat the question and ask them to share their thoughts in a sentence or two. Anyone who wishes to pass may do so.

Warming Up
5-10 minutes

Center yourself by breathing in and out several times. Relax your neck and then take time to let your other muscles relax. Offer distracting thoughts to God, one by one. Ask yourself the following question to help focus your thoughts for the meditation: What, if anything, do I think God may have been telling me this week?

Close your eyes and take a few minutes to reflect on this question, pondering the events of the week, conversations with friends, books you've read. See if anything comes to you. If not, that's fine. Simply enjoy the presence of God.

Reading the Passage
15-20 minutes

Read silently the following passage, noting the explanations in the shaded box.

---

❶ Ask a group member to read the Scripture passage aloud. Suggest that other group members close their eyes as they listen.

Matthew 7:7-11

TRUSTING GOD

⁷Ask and it will be given to you; seek and you will find; knock and the door will be opened to you. ⁸For everyone who asks receives; he who seeks finds; and to him who knocks, the door will be opened.

THE KIND OF FATHER GOD IS

⁹"Which of you, if his son asks for *bread, will give him a stone?* ¹⁰Or if he asks for a *fish, will give him a snake?* [Or if he asks for an *egg, will give him a scorpion?* Luke 11:12] ¹¹If you, then, though you are evil, know how to give *good gifts* to your children, how much more will your Father in heaven give good gifts to those who ask him!

If you haven't read the notes in the shaded box, read them silently now. Take a minute to consider the following questions.

> ❶ After the passage is read, ask group members to read silently the explanations in the shaded box and then jot down answers to the questions below. After a few minutes, have them choose one question and share their answer in a sentence or two. Anyone who wishes to pass may do so. Explain that this is not a time for discussion but for reporting responses to the questions.

Asking, Seeking, Knocking

1. This passage has sometimes been viewed as a recipe for getting what we want from God rather than as instruction on what kind of heart to have. What kind of heart do Jesus' words urge us to have?

2. Based on this passage, what words would you use to describe the parent-heart of God?

3. Verse 8 has been interpreted to mean that if you ask God for something, you will get it. As a result, people feel injured by God because of unanswered prayers and longings. Asking, seeking, and knocking imply conversation with God that's more intricate and involved than *God, please give me _____*. Think

---

Bread . . . stone—The little, round, limestone stones on the seashore were similar in shape and color to bread loaves of that day.

Fish . . . snake—"Snake" probably refers to an eel, which was deemed unclean in Jewish dietary laws and was a sneaky, forbidden substitute for a fish.

Egg . . . scorpion—A stinging scorpion, which is potentially fatal, looks like an egg when it's curled up in a ball and is pale in color.

Good gifts—The parallel passage in Luke uses the words "Holy Spirit" instead of good gifts. Jesus probably taught this several times, and once when He did, He mentioned specifically the gift of the Holy Spirit.

of something you have asked God for (perhaps related to a goal, relationship, or job) and write some questions you can ask God, since you have a relationship with Him in which you can ask, seek, and knock.

4. Which of these asking-seeking-knocking questions would you like to pose to God concerning your purpose here on earth?

☐ What next?
☐ Who should I be listening to?
☐ Which direction should I take?
☐ What have you put in my heart to do?
☐ Your question:

☐ Your question:

Content Consideration

5. This discourse falls between a section on avoiding judging others and another on choosing the narrow door. The first asks us to be merciful and the other points us toward integrity. How does an asking-seeking-knocking heart help build mercy and integrity in us?

Picturing the Passage   10-15 minutes

Before reading the passage again, consider this cue.

Character Cue: Jesus' Use of Absurdity in Teaching

Jesus did a good job of making unforgettable points with absurd examples. For example, the prodigal son story began with the absurd idea that a son might say, "Dad, let's pretend you're dead. I'll take my half now." Jesus told another parable about two brothers who couldn't get their intentions and behavior straight: one said he'd work in the vineyard, but didn't; the other said he wouldn't, but did (Matthew 21:27-31). Another time, Jesus compared the learned Pharisees to people who think nothing of drinking out of a dirty cup because, well, it's immaculately clean on the outside, isn't it? (Matthew 23:25-26).

In Matthew 7:7-11, Jesus' absurd comparisons were designed to help people think, *Of course God isn't like that! God isn't a sneaky trickster or an inattentive parent who would give us the wrong thing when we ask.* Imagine the good feelings about God that Jesus' listeners must have had after they'd laughed at Jesus' absurd word pictures.

Now read the passage aloud and close your eyes, picturing the comparisons Jesus made (listed in the shaded box) and the passion involved in trying to explain to humans the love of God.

❶ Have group members read this cue silently. Then ask a group member to read the passage aloud while the others picture the comparisons.

Soaking In the Passage   5-15 minutes
Consider how in the midst of your everyday events this passage touches your life today. Read the passage aloud again and ponder the following question for several minutes: *What word or picture emerges from the passage and stays with me?* It often helps to close your eyes in order to shut out distractions.

After several minutes, write down the words or pictures that resonate within you from the passage.

Words:

Pictures: I hear . . . I see . . .

❶ Have a different group member read the passage aloud and then state the question printed in italics. After the group sits quietly for a few minutes, ask each group member to read what they've written.

Pondering the Invitation   5-15 minutes
Perhaps God is offering you an invitation in this passage to do or be something within the next few days. What might that be? Reflect quietly for a few moments, pondering this question: *What do I sense this passage calling me to consider?*

❶ Read the above instructions aloud and after a few minutes, repeat the question printed in italics. Ask group members to respond by saying, "I sense this passage calling me to consider. . . ." Then complete that statement with a short phrase. Anyone who wishes to pass may do so.

Praying   5-10 minutes

Take a few minutes to respond to God by telling Him what you sensed or didn't sense during this meditation. If you need to present questions to God, do so.

❶ After allowing a few minutes for private prayer, ask group members to pray for the person on their right. Anyone wishing to pray silently may do so by saying, "I'm praying silently," and signifying when he or she is finished by saying "Amen."

Daily Lectio

Use the above format to enjoy God's presence between group meetings, using any of the following passages:

- Psalm 24:1-6 (the generation of those who seek Him)
- Psalm 105:1-5 (seeking God's face always)
- Psalm 138:1-8 (God will fulfill His purpose)
- Isaiah 65:19-24 (promise of renewal)
- Amos 5:14 (the Lord is with us when we seek good instead of evil)
- Acts 17:26-28 (God's design that we seek Him)

Giving Up What Hinders Me
Mark 10:17-25

❶ After your group has had a chance to greet each other, read the centering instructions in the "Warming Up" section. Then ask the quiet question. Sit quietly together for a few minutes, repeat the question, and ask group members to share their thoughts in a sentence or two. Anyone who wishes to pass may do so.

Warming Up   5-10 minutes
Center yourself by breathing in and out several times. Relax your neck and then take time to let your other muscles relax. If you feel distracted, jot down anything you need to remember and begin turning concerns over to God. Ask yourself the following question to help focus your thoughts for meditation on today's passage: Who has done a good job of looking at me with an expression of love (not in the romantic sense)? Close your eyes and reflect on your past experiences or pressing needs in your life.

Reading the Passage   15-20 minutes
Read silently the following passage, noting the explanations in the shaded box.

❶ Ask a group member to read the Scripture passage aloud. Suggest that other group members close their eyes as they listen.

Mark 10:17-25

FIRST QUESTION
¹⁷As Jesus started on his way, *a man* ran up to him and fell on his knees before him. "Good teacher," he asked, "what must I do to inherit eternal life?"

[18]"Why do you call me good?" Jesus answered. "No one is good—except God alone. [19]You know the commandments: *'Do not* murder, do not commit adultery, do not steal, do not give false testimony, do not defraud, honor your father and mother.'"

SECOND QUESTION

[20]"Teacher," he declared, "all these I have kept since I was a boy." ["What do I still lack?" Matthew 19:20b]

[21]Jesus looked at him and loved him. "One thing you lack," he said. *"Go, sell everything you have and give to the poor,* and you will have treasure in heaven. Then come, follow me." [22]At this the man's face fell. He went away sad, because he had great wealth.

JESUS' WARNING

[23]Jesus looked around and said to his disciples, "How hard it is for the rich to enter the kingdom of God!" [24]The disciples were amazed at his words. But Jesus said again, "Children, how hard it is to enter the kingdom of God! [25]It is easier for a camel to go through the eye of a needle than for a rich man to enter the kingdom of God."

If you haven't read the notes in the shaded box, read them now. Take a minute to consider the following questions.

❶ After the passage is read, ask group members to read silently the explanations in the shaded box and jot down answers to the questions below. After a few minutes, have them choose one question and share their answer in a sentence or two. Anyone who wishes to pass may do so. Remind them that this is not a time for discussion but for reporting responses to the questions.

The Rich Young Ruler

1. The text doesn't tell us why the rich young ruler was sad. If his thoughts and feelings were like the kind you have, why would he have been sad? (Check as many as you like.)

   ☐ He wanted so much to be righteous.
   ☐ He wanted to be with God eternally.

A man—This man was young (Matthew 19:20, 22) and a ruler of some kind (Luke 18:18).

Do not . . .—Jesus named the commandments that describe interpersonal relationships.

Go, sell everything . . . —Jesus did not say this often, except to this man and to His disciples (Luke 12:33).

☐ His riches meant too much to him.
☐ He was shocked that Jesus required him to sell his possessions for the poor.
☐ Giving everything to the poor seemed like a silly idea.
☐ Living in poverty as Jesus often did had little appeal for him.
☐ Other:

Jesus' Warning

As you ponder this passage, consider that you may be among the "rich in this present world" who are commanded to do good and to be generous (1 Timothy 6:17-18). If you can afford a house or apartment, possessions to fill it, and food more costly than rice and beans, you're "rich" compared to most people living on this planet.

2. Reflect on why it's difficult for the rich to enter the kingdom of God. What do possessions and spending power have to do with spirituality?

3. Jesus "looked at him and loved him" before giving him terribly difficult commands: "Go, sell everything you have and give to the poor, and you will have treasure in heaven. Then come, follow me" (verse 21). Based on what you know about the heart of Christ, why do you think Jesus may have offered that look of love?

   ☐ to soften the blow
   ☐ to encourage the man that the sacrifice would be worth it
   ☐ to offer the man love, even though he would refuse the challenge
   ☐ to keep the door open, as if to say, "Come back, young man, when you're ready"
   ☐ other:

Treasure in Heaven

4. Ponder what the phrase "treasure in heaven" means. It is used in the following ways:

   ■ Jesus looked at him and loved him. "One thing you lack," he said. "Go, sell everything you have and give to the poor, and you will have *treasure in heaven*. Then come, follow me" (Mark 10:21, emphasis added).
   ■ "But store up for yourselves *treasures in heaven,* where moth and rust do not destroy, and where thieves do not break in and steal. For where your *treasure* is, there your heart will be also" (Matthew 6:20-21, emphasis added). (Context: Jesus just spoke about fasting, and after this verse, He talks about the eye being the lamp of the body.)

The word *treasure* is used in the following ways:

- The kingdom of heaven is like *treasure* hidden in a field. When a man found it, he hid it again, and then in his joy went and sold all he had and bought that field (Matthew 13:44, emphasis added).
- My purpose is that they may be encouraged in heart and united in love, so that they may have the full riches of complete understanding, in order that they may know the mystery of God, namely Christ, in whom are hidden all the *treasures* of wisdom and knowledge (Colossians 2:2-3, emphasis added).
- In this way they will lay up *treasure* for themselves as a firm foundation for the coming age, so that they may take hold of the life that is truly life (1 Timothy 6:19). (This verse follows the command that the "rich in this present world" are to do good and to be generous, cited above.)

What treasure in heaven could possibly be so great that people would sell all their earthly possessions to get it?

5. If Jesus were to confront you in a moment when you were excited about obeying Him, and He were to ask you to give up something too dear, what might that be?

☐ a compulsive behavior — spending, eating
☐ attention to outward appearance — nice clothing and so on
☐ possessions
☐ academic achievement, career achievement, achievement of your child or spouse
☐ other: the need to . . .
☐ other:

Picturing the Passage   10-15 minutes
Before reading the passage again, consider these cues.

Character Cue: The Rich Young Ruler
"Who was this man? The word *young* means that he would have been between twenty-four and forty years old. To say that he was a ruler probably meant that he was a member of the Sanhedrin . . . , the highest Jewish authority in all of Palestine. The man must have been unusually devout in his faith if he was a member of this important council at such a young age."[1]

"Most wealthy men of that day rode in chariots drawn by their own horses and owned a lot of land and slaves. Their houses were filled with expensive furniture and beautiful rugs in a variety of colors. They wore white wool or silk robes, and their wives wore embroidered linen and bracelets, necklaces, and armbands of gold and silver. Middle-class society was rare in Israel during New Testament times. A few families lived in great wealth; most had almost nothing. A tremendous gap existed between rich and poor, and as a result the poor were exploited."[2]

Cultural Cue: Eye of Needle

This term commonly refers to the hole in the top portion of a sewing needle. In biblical times, sewing needles looked as they do now, except they were made of bronze or iron. Try to get a mental picture of a huge camel facing a tiny needle and trying to fit through the needle's eye. Many readers of this passage have found this image so preposterous that they have proposed alternate meanings: the Needle's Eye was a gate in Jerusalem, for example. However, there is simply no evidence for any of these proposals.[3]

Now that you've looked at these cues, take a few minutes to quiet yourself again and read the passage aloud this time. Close your eyes, picturing this young man and his interaction with Jesus.

> ❶ Have group members read these cues silently. Then ask a group member read the passage aloud while the others picture the passage.

Soaking In the Passage   5-15 minutes

Reflect on how this passage touches your life today by pondering this question: *What words or scenes emerge from the passage and stay with me?* If you begin to latch on to something that is most evident, step back a minute and wait to see if anything else emerges.

After a few minutes, write down the words or scenes that resonate within you from the passage.

Words:

Scene: I hear . . . I see . . .

> ❶ Have a different group member read the passage aloud and then state the question printed in italics. After the group sits quietly for a few minutes, have each write down the word or image that stays with him or her. Ask group members to read what they've written.

Pondering the Invitation   5-15 minutes

Perhaps God is offering you an invitation in this passage to do or be or know something within the next few days. What might that be? God may be asking you, "Where is your heart—in possessions? In what other thing?" Sit quietly for a few minutes, pondering this question: *What do I need to know from this passage?* Don't feel pressured to come up with an insight right away.

❶ Read the instructions aloud, and after a few minutes, repeat the question printed in italics. Ask group members to respond by saying, "I sense this passage telling me to. . . ." Then complete that statement with a short phrase. Anyone who wishes to pass may do so.

Praying   5-10 minutes

Take a few minutes to respond to God about this passage. How do you feel about what you sensed (or didn't sense)? What is it you most want to say to God at this time?

❶ After allowing a few minutes for private prayer, ask group members to pray for the person on their left. Anyone wishing to pray silently may do so by saying, "I'm praying silently," then signifying when he or she is finished by saying "Amen."

Daily Lectio

If you wish, use the above format to meditate on God's Word between group meetings. You may wish to focus on today's passage every day this week, or you can use the following passages:

- Matthew 6:20-21 (references to "treasure in heaven")
- Matthew 13:44 (the kingdom of heaven is like a treasure hidden in a field)
- Luke 12:16-21 (the parable of the greedy farmer)
- Luke 12:30-34 (Jesus' command to disciples to sell their possessions)
- 1 Timothy 6:6-10 (love of money is the root of evil)
- 1 Timothy 6:17-19 (lay up treasure as a firm foundation)

---

1. V. Gilbert Beers, *The Victor Journey Through the Bible* (Wheaton, Ill.: Victor Books, 1986), p. 297.
2. Beers, p. 291
3. Gordon D. Fee and Douglas Stuart. *How to Read the Bible for All Its Worth* (Grand Rapids, Mich.: Zondervan, 1981, 1993), p. 21.

Exploring God's Purposes For Me

Philippians 3:8,10-11; Colossians 2:2-3;
1 Thessalonians 2:11-12,19-20

> ❶ After group members have had a chance to greet each other, read the centering instructions in the "Warming Up" section. Before reading the prayer aloud, ask the quiet question printed in italics. Then read the prayer and let group members reflect for a few minutes. Repeat the question and ask them to share their thoughts in a sentence or two. Anyone who wishes to pass may do so.

Warming Up · 5-10 minutes

Center yourself by breathing in and out several times. Relax your neck and then take time to let your other muscles relax. Set aside each thought that distracts you. Then read aloud this prayer penned by Florence Nightingale and sit in the quiet. If you wish, read it aloud again.

> Oh God, you put into my heart this great desire to devote myself to the sick and sorrowful; I offer it to you. Do with it what is for your service. . . . O Lord, even now I am trying to snatch the management of your world from your hands. Too little have I looked for something higher and better than my own work—the work of supreme Wisdom, which uses us whether we know it or not.[1]

Reflect for a moment. Which phrase from the prayer (if any) speaks to me in my situation?

Reading the Passages 15-20 minutes

Read silently the following passages, noting the explanations in the shaded box.

> ❶ Ask a group member to read the Scripture passages. Suggest that other group members close their eyes as they listen.

Philippians 3:8, 10-11

GOALS WORTH LOSING EVERYTHING ELSE

[8]I consider *everything* a loss compared to the surpassing greatness of knowing Christ Jesus my Lord, for whose sake I have lost all things. . . . [10]I want to know Christ and the power of his resurrection and the fellowship of sharing in his sufferings, becoming like him in his death, [11]and so, somehow, to attain to the resurrection from the dead.

Colossians 2:2-3

RELATIONSHIPS AND HOW PAUL VIEWED THEM

[2]My purpose is that *they* may be encouraged in heart and united in love, so that they may have the full riches of complete understanding, in order that they may know the mystery of God, namely, Christ, [3]in whom are hidden all the treasures of wisdom and knowledge.

1 Thessalonians 2:11-12,19-20

[11]For you know that we dealt with *each of you* as a father deals with his own children, [12]encouraging, comforting and urging *you* to live lives worthy of God, who calls *you* into his kingdom and glory. . . . [19]For what is our hope, our joy, or the crown in which we will glory in the presence of our Lord Jesus when he comes? Is it not *you?* [20]Indeed, *you* are our glory and joy.

If you haven't read the notes in the shaded box, read them silently now. Take a minute to consider the following questions.

Everything—Paul, the missionary-writer of these verses, was probably referring back to verses 4-6, in which he listed the high credentials he had as a Jewish leader before he became a Christian. Since his conversion, he had traveled extensively, giving up family and leisure. He wrote these words from a prison cell, and so he had also given up his freedom.

They—The Colossians had been subject to heretical teachings about Christ, which had caused a lot of confusion and, no doubt, hurt.

Each of you—The Thessalonian converts were young Christians who had undergone persecution (1:6; 3:1-4,7-8).

❶ After the passages are read, ask group members to read silently the explanations in the shaded box and then jot down answers to the questions below. After a few minutes, have each choose one question and share his or her answer to that question in a sentence or two. Anyone who wishes to pass may do so. Explain that this is not a time for discussion but for reporting responses to the questions.

Paul's Purpose in Life

1. In the first passage, notice the emphasis on the words: *Christ, Lord,* and *Jesus.* How would you describe Paul's purpose in relation to God?

   ■ How did that relationship with God affect other things in life?
   ■ How did it affect his willingness to suffer?

2. In the second and third passages, look at the places where the words *they, each of you,* and *you* occur. Paul was talking about the people he served. How would you describe Paul's purpose as it related to other people?

Purpose in Life Affects Service

3. Paul also wrote this phrase, "For to me, to live is Christ" (Philippians 1:21). In Eugenia Price's book, *Discoveries,* she explored the substitute reasons for living listed below. Check the ones you have dabbled in at times:

   ☐ For me to live is . . . to be religious.
   ☐ For me to live is . . . to serve other people.
   ☐ For me to live is . . . to serve Christ.
   ☐ For me to live is . . . to be Christlike.[2]

   What is the difference between living for Christ and living to be like Christ?

4. Paul was a doer, yet he valued knowing Christ above all else. The paradox is that knowing Christ affects everything else. If you were to value Christ above all else, which of the below areas would be affected? (Check as many boxes as you wish.)

   ☐ my choice of service
   ☐ my attitudes toward coworkers
   ☐ my attitude toward my own service
   ☐ my attitude toward church
   ☐ other area:

Picturing the Passage   10-15 minutes
Before reading the passage again, consider these cues.

Character and Setting Cues: Paul in Prison

The apostle Paul spent some time in dark prison cells (where he may not have had a toilet or been offered food and water, but relied on outsiders to provide it). But when he wrote Philippians and Colossians, his prison was a house where he was kept under close guard at all times and was probably chained to a soldier. He was given certain freedoms not offered to most prisoners. He was allowed to write letters and see any visitors he wanted to see.[3]

Still, what could be a worse situation for a missionary called to travel the Roman Empire planting churches? From the book of Acts, we see that he was good at spearheading movements for Christ in towns that worshiped all kinds of idols. How could he be "wasted" in a Roman prison?

Imagine this intelligent man who had experienced the thrill of missionary work cooped up in a house with Roman guards, wanting desperately to make known the name of Christ to the world. Imagine him closing his eyes and reflecting on the Thessalonians as his hope, joy, and crown in which he would glory in the presence of the Lord Jesus.

Armed with these cues, read the passages aloud and then close your eyes and ponder one or two of these phrases:

- to know Christ
- the power of His resurrection
- fellowship of sharing in His sufferings
- becoming like Him in His death
- have full riches of complete understanding
- know the mystery of God
- Christ, in whom are hidden all the treasures of wisdom and knowledge

Or, ponder verse 19, "For what is our hope, our joy, or the crown in which we will glory in the presence of our Lord Jesus when he comes? Is it not you?" Picture someone who is your hope, joy, and crown, in whom you'll glory.

> ❶ Have group members read these cues and suggestions silently. Then have a group member read the Scripture passages aloud while the others ponder one of the phrases.

Soaking In the Passages   5-15 minutes

Reflect now on how these Scripture passages touch your life today. Read the passages aloud again and ponder the following question for several minutes: *What word, phrase, or image emerges from the passages and stays with me?* If you begin to latch on to something that is most evident, step back a minute and wait to see if anything else emerges.

After several minutes, write down the words or images that resonate with you from the passages. Or, if you wish, try drawing or doodling an abstract symbol or visual image. Engage yourself in it, and then sit quietly with it.

Word or phrase:

Image: I hear . . . I see . . .

❶ Have a different group member read the passages aloud and then state the question printed in italics. Ask the group to sit quietly for a while and then write the words or images that come to mind. After a few minutes, ask group members to read what they've written. Anyone who wishes to pass may do so.

Pondering the Invitation   5-15 minutes
Perhaps God is offering you an invitation in these passages to do or be something within the next few days. What might that be? Sit in silence for a few minutes, pondering this question: *What do I sense this passage calling me to understand or to do differently?*

❶ Read the above instructions aloud and, after a few minutes, repeat the question printed in italics. Ask group members to respond by saying, "I sense this passage calling me to . . ." Then complete that statement with a short phrase. Anyone who wishes to pass may do so.

Praying   5-10 minutes
Respond to God by telling Him how you feel about what you sensed or didn't sense during this meditation. What do you most want to say to God at this time? If you need to present questions to God, do so.

❶ After allowing a few minutes for private prayer, ask group members to pray for the person on their left. Anyone wishing to pray silently may do so, saying, "I'm praying silently," then signifying when he or she is finished by saying "Amen."

Daily Lectio
If you wish, use the above format to meditate on God's Word between group meetings. You may wish to focus on today's passages every day this week, or you can use the following passages:

- 1 Corinthians 3:6-10 (about sharing purpose with others)
- Ephesians 1:12, 2:14-16 (God's purpose in reconciling people to Him and to each other)
- Philippians 1:21-26 (Paul's purpose to live for Christ)
- Philippians 2:12-13 (God working in us for a purpose, written from prison)
- 1 Thessalonians 2:4-7 (Paul's integrity in his service to others)
- 1 Thessalonians 2:11-12 (Paul's caring manner in serving others)

---

1. Florence Nightingale, as quoted in Veronica Zundel, ed., *The Eerdmans Book of Famous Prayers* (Grand Rapids, Mich.: Eerdmans, 1983), p. 76.
2. Eugenia Price, *Discoveries* (Grand Rapids, Mich.: Zondervan, 1970), pp. 47, 51, 55, 59.
3. *Life Application Bible* (Wheaton, Ill.: Tyndale, 1991), p. 2158.

God Puts Passion in My Heart

Nehemiah 1:2-4,11; 2:2-5,8b,11-12,15a,17-18

❶ After group members have had a chance to greet each other, read the centering instructions in the "Warming Up" section. Then present the quiet question, read the prayer, and let group members reflect quietly for a few minutes. Repeat the question and ask them to name the image that resonates with them.

Warming Up   5-10 minutes

Center yourself by breathing in and out several times. Relax your neck and then take time to let your other muscles relax. Set aside your distractions by turning them over to God one by one. Then read the prayer below and ask yourself, What image in this prayer resonates most with me?

GOD THE ARTIST
BY DAG HAMMARSKJOLD
You take the pen,
and the lines dance.
You take the flute,
and the notes shimmer.
You take the brush,
and the colours sing.
So all things have meaning and beauty
in that space beyond time where you are.
How, then, can I hold back anything from you.[1]

Reading the Passage   15-20 minutes
As you read, enter into an ancient world of exiles who believed in God, even though they had been defeated and lived in a pagan nation. Read silently the following Scripture passage, noting the explanations in the shaded boxes.

❶ Ask a group member to read the Scripture passage aloud. Suggest that other group members close their eyes as they listen.

Nehemiah 1:2-4,11; 2:2-5,8b,11-12,15a,17-18
(Nehemiah speaking)

WEEPING FOR THE HOMELAND

1:2Hanani, one of my brothers, came from Judah with some other men, and I questioned them about the *Jewish remnant that survived the exile,* and also about Jerusalem.

3They said to me, "Those who survived the exile and are *back in the province* are in great trouble and disgrace. The wall of Jerusalem is broken down, and its gates have been *burned with fire.*"

4When I heard these things, *I sat down and wept.* For some days I mourned and fasted and prayed before the God of heaven. . . . 11I was *cupbearer* to *the king.*

INTERACTING WITH THE KING

2:2The king asked me, "Why does your face look so sad when you are not ill? This can be nothing but sadness of heart."

I was very *much afraid,* 3but I said to the king, "May the king live forever! Why should my face not look sad when the city where my fathers are buried lies in ruins, and its gates have been destroyed by fire?"

4The king said to me, "What is it you want?"

Then I *prayed to the God of heaven,* 5and I answered the king, "If it pleases the king and if your servant has found favor in his sight, let him send me to the city in Judah where my fathers are buried so that I can rebuild it." 8bAnd because the gracious hand of my God was upon me, the king granted my requests.

INSPECTING THE WALL

2:11I went to Jerusalem, and after staying there three days 12aI set out during the night with a few men. I had not told anyone what my God

---

Jewish remnant that survived the exile—Throughout Israel's history, God warned that they would be taken captive by another nation if they continued to live wickedly and worship idols. Judah, the southern kingdom, was taken into exile by Babylonia in 586 B.C. A few Israelites (remnant) were left behind.

Back in the province—After seventy years, two waves of exiles returned, led by Zerubbabel and Ezra.

Burned with fire—The Babylonians had besieged and burned the city. A small group had tried to rebuild the walls, but the neighboring Samaritans stopped them.

I sat down and wept—Nehemiah lived far from his Jewish homeland in exile. He cared about Jerusalem's welfare because he was afraid that Judah would stray from God again without walls for defense and a stronger commitment to God.   *continued*

had put in my heart to do for Jerusalem ¹⁵ªso I went up the valley by night, examining the wall.

IMPARTING THE VISION

²:¹⁷Then I said to them [the officials], "You see the trouble we are in: Jerusalem lies in ruins, and its gates have been burned with fire. Come, let us rebuild the wall of Jerusalem, and we will no longer be in disgrace." ¹⁸I also told them about the gracious hand of my God upon me and what the king had said to me. They replied, "Let us start rebuilding."

Result: The wall of Jerusalem was rebuilt in fifty-two days (Nehemiah 6:15).

If you haven't read the notes in the shaded boxes, read them silently now. Take a minute to consider the following questions.

> ❶ After the passage is read, ask group members to read the explanations in the shaded boxes and then jot down answers to the questions below. After a few minutes, have each choose one question and share his or her answer in a sentence or two. Anyone who wishes to pass may do so. Remind them that this is not a time for discussion but for reporting responses to the questions.

Nehemiah, the Politician from a Foreign Land

1. Nehemiah had probably lived his entire life in Babylon or Susa, the capital of Persia. He had an important job and, probably, a lot of respect. It's difficult to understand why his homeland meant so much to him, except that God put it in his heart. What people or group of people are experiencing brokenness, breaking your heart when you ponder their plight—even though it may be remote from your experience?

Cupbearer—This position was something like the U.S. Secret Service, which protects the President. Nehemiah taste-tested the king's food and drink to foil assassination plots. He had to be completely trustworthy, above taking a bribe.

The king—King Darius of Persia. After the Jews were taken captive, the Persians captured the Babylonians, and Jews like Nehemiah could be found serving the Persian king.

Much afraid—Servants, no matter how trusted, did not bother the king with their problems. Nor did they make bold requests for permission and provisions for a cause their master had already outlawed (Ezra 4:17-22).

Prayed to the God of heaven—Throughout this narrative, Nehemiah can be found praying in all kinds of situations.

2. In what place in your life do you feel like an exile, estranged from who you are and the purposes God has for you?

Nehemiah, the Leader

3. Nehemiah's goal came to pass, in part, because he allowed God to infuse in him a sense of purpose—"what God put in my heart to do." Nehemiah's strong sense of purpose is evident by the following items:

   - his weeping over the homeland
   - his inspection of the wall by night
   - his emphasis on the "gracious hand of my God" (2:8,18)
   - his powerful persuasion of the officials

   How do the first two items differ from useless brooding?

4. Nehemiah's passion was exhibited by how he wept, prayed, and followed through. Think about the things you're passionate about. Check any of the items below that you need to do more of concerning the causes God has put in your heart.

   ☐ experiencing others' brokenness and getting involved emotionally, weeping over it
   ☐ praying for God's wisdom and insight, confessing my lack of finesse
   ☐ doing something, even if it's insignificant, to work on the situation

Picturing the Passage   10-15 minutes
Before reading the passage again, consider this cue.

Cultural Cue: Nehemiah as a Politician
Review the "cupbearer" note in the shaded box on page 217. Because Nehemiah held an important rank, he probably dressed well and had servants waiting on him.

Consider how Nehemiah may have felt when he saw Jerusalem's crumbled walls. He worked and probably lived in the two palaces of King Darius the Great. Besides the summer palace in Susa, the winter palace in Persepolis had a flat terrace with seventy-two great columns, some of which were sixty-five feet high, topped by carvings of bulls and horned lions. The palace and city were surrounded by three separate walls carved with elaborate figures and protected by many watch-towers.[2]

Now read the passage aloud and close your eyes, picturing the events as if they were a movie playing in your mind. You may wish to choose one or more of these scenes to picture:

- *weeping for the homeland:* Imagine Nehemiah asking them specifically about the welfare of the people left in Jerusalem and what the city looked like.
- *interacting with the king (four months later):* Imagine Nehemiah's fear as he risked personal and political rejection.
- *inspecting the walls:* Imagine Nehemiah going at night with just a few men to survey the damage.
- *imparting the vision to the officials:* Imagine the pressure he felt. The king of Persia had championed this idea, which was a miracle. How did the officials of this outland province view Nehemiah, who may have behaved more like a Persian than a Jew? Did they resent him as a representative of an oppressive power, evidenced everywhere by military camps? Or had these officials become used to the broken walls? With one attempt already defeated, did they wonder, *Who is this guy and why does he bother?*

❶ Ask group members to read the cue and information silently. Then have someone read the passage aloud while the others picture it.

Soaking In the Passage

5-15 minutes

Ponder how your life is touched by this passage today. Read the passage aloud again and consider this question for several minutes: *What words or dramatic moments emerge from the passage and stay with me?*

After several minutes, record the words or scenes that resonate with you from the passage.

Words:

Moments: I hear . . . I see . . .

❶ Have a different group member read the passage aloud and then state the question printed in italics. Have the group sit quietly for a while and then record the words or images that stay with them. After a few minutes, ask group members to read what they've written. Anyone who wishes to pass may do so.

Pondering the Invitation

5-15 minutes

Perhaps God is offering you an invitation in this passage to do or be something within the next few days. What might that be? Sit in silence for a few minutes, pondering this question: *What do I sense this passage calling me to do or be right now?*

❶ Read the above instructions aloud. After a few minutes, repeat the question printed in italics. Ask group members to respond by saying, "I sense this passage calling me to. . . ." Then complete that statement with a short phrase. Anyone who wishes to pass may do so.

Praying   5-10 minutes

Take a few minutes to respond to God about this meditation. How do you feel about what you sensed (or didn't sense)? What do you most want to say to God at this time?

❶ After allowing a few minutes for private prayer, ask group members to pray for the person on their left. Anyone wishing to pray silently may do so by saying, "I'm praying silently," and signifying when he or she is finished by saying "Amen."

Daily Lectio

If you wish, use the above format to meditate on God's Word between group meetings. You may wish to focus on today's passage every day this week, or you can use the following passages:

- 1 Chronicles 22:6-12 (David wants to build the temple, but it wasn't to be)
- Nehemiah 1:5-11 (one of Nehemiah's prayers)
- Nehemiah 4:4-9 (Nehemiah prays in the midst of his troublemakers)
- Nehemiah 6:9-15 (Nehemiah prays in the midst of his troublemakers)
- Proverbs 19:20-21 (differences between our plans and God's purpose)
- Colossians 2:2-3 (one of Paul's statements of purpose)

---

1. Dag Hammarskjold, "God the Artist" as quoted in Zundel, p. 95.
2. V. Gilbert Beers, *The Victor Journey Through the Bible* (Wheaton, Ill.: Victor Books, 1986), pp. 64-65.